Emotional Intelligence 101

Boost Your EQ For More Emotional Agility, Spirituality, Better Relationships, Success and Power - Achieve Mastery of Fear, Anger, Joy, Happiness, Persuasion and Social Skills

Tobias Entwistle

All Copyrights Reserved.

TABLE OF CONTENTS

INTRODUCTION 1

CHAPTER ONE : WHAT IS EMOTIONAL INTELLIGENCE? (DEFINITIONS AND CONCEPTS) 4

CHAPTER TWO : IDENTIFYING AND IMPROVING EMOTIONAL INTELLIGENCE IN YOURSELF AND IN OTHERS AROUND YOU 17

CHAPTER THREE : SECRETS TO BOOSTING YOUR SPIRITUALITY AND TAPPING INTO AN ENDLESS AMOUNT OF JOY 30

CHAPTER FOUR : PROVEN EMOTIONAL INTELLIGENCE STRATEGIES TO DRIVE YOUR SUCCESS, POWER, AND MOTIVATION 42

CHAPTER FIVE : HOW YOU CAN BOOST YOUR EMOTIONAL INTELLIGENCE ALMOST OVERNIGHT 55

CHAPTER SIX : 7 TIPS TO INCREASE YOUR EQ FOR BETTER RELATIONSHIPS 67

CHAPTER SEVEN : 19 WAYS TO IMPROVE YOUR EMOTIONS IN 2019 81

CHAPTER EIGHT : THE LITTLE-KNOWN TIME-TESTED PRINCIPLES TO FOLLOW IF YOU WANT TO PERSUADE OTHERS 103

CHAPTER NINE : THE DARK SIDE OF EMOTIONAL INTELLIGENCE... 113

CHAPTER TEN : DOES EMOTIONAL INTELLIGENCE REALLY EXIST? (NOW YOU KNOW BETTER) 123

CONCLUSION 129

Introduction

To begin with, we all have at least an iota of this kind of intelligence in us, whether we acknowledge it or not. Emotional Intelligence goes beyond perceiving our emotions as a tool for making us weak. As a matter of fact, it is the total means of identifying, notifying, and making good use of our emotions to our own advantage.

It is important to know that a great deal can be gained from exploring our Emotional Intelligence. If we can tweak our emotions appropriately, we will not only be immune to a negative impact but also encourage success and growth in our lives. Many years ago, I was also a novice as regards this concept. In fact, I didn't know Emotional Intelligence existed at all. When I was mad and followed the dictates of my emotions, I didn't know I was blindly following my emotions.

I didn't know I was allowing my emotions to influence my decisions. Even when I was overwhelmed or extremely happy, I didn't know emotions could be quite detrimental in the decisions we make in the moment. But, when I came across a book that enlightened me about the world of Emotional Intelligence, I knew it was only a matter of time before I would start writing amazing content about it.

I knew it was only a matter of time before would I share my ideas on Emotional Intelligence with everyone around me. Well, we are here, aren't we? Emotional Intelligence deals with the ability to control your own emotions by having control of the outcome. Think about it - we really can't stop ourselves from the feelings that run through our body. These feelings are a result of our inner thoughts, wants, or desires, which are triggered by the outside forces.

So the question remains - if we cannot stop ourselves from feeling that way, what then can we do to manage those feelings? Emotional Intelligence is the answer you would always arrive at. Now, this is the message I bring with this book. What this book will do is to familiarize you with the values and principles, as well as tenets of Emotional Intelligence.

In the end, we will realize that our emotions will lead us astray most of the time. Whoever follows his or her emotions all the time ends up making a mess of his or herself. This is why great men always have a high level of Emotional Intelligence. Thanks to Emotional Intelligence, they can easily keep their emotions in check without the slightest issue. Believe it or not, a master of Emotional Intelligence is liked by all.

When you understand as well as respect others' emotions, you are bound to be loved. You are bound to be held in high esteem. A lot of these people around you will want to connect with you because they believe you are a great person with empathy and compassion. You will be able to build relationships and even earn the respect of everyone around you.

Be that as it may, read through the chapters of this book, so as to learn the real meaning of Emotional Intelligence. Allow me to take you through my journey toward becoming a master of Emotional Intelligence, as well as the outstanding benefits it has afforded.

Chapter One

What is Emotional Intelligence? (Definitions and Concepts)

It is important to know that the phrase "what is" contains lots of compelling ideas fused into one. "What is" does not only mean what defines a concept or an idea; it goes way beyond that. It encompasses scintillating and a wide range of thoughts concerning that concept or idea. Now, "What is Emotional Intelligence" is a very deep question. As a matter of fact, if we are to start delving into this question, the whole book won't be enough. Thus, we will be as concise as possible.

The question now is, "What is Emotional Intelligence?" We wouldn't be entirely wrong to we say emotions have been present since the beginning of time. Man was created to be clueless and emotion-free, until they ate the forbidden fruit in the Garden of Eden. Ever since then, man's eyes have been opened to the realities around him - and these new abilities of theirs came with emotions and feelings.

They now know their left from right. They bonded with their environment and could feel it. The first men started learning about the real meaning of emotions. Lots of questions had also gone through their minds; questions like why would they cry at a painful situation? Why would they feel happy when their purposes seemed to be fulfilled? Why feel anguish and grief when they lose someone close? These kinds of questions had been a mystery to them.

However, as time progressed, humans evolved. Emotions, over time, became better understood with lots of research, studies, and surveys carried out all through this era. In recent times, humans have mastered emotions to a large extent. Now, many people in the world today can easily tame their emotions, or show an expressionless demeanor even when battling with raging emotions inside of them.

The art of Emotional Intelligence can be said to be quite similar to Stoicism. With both synonymous to emotional control, one can boldly say that a true stoic is a master of Emotional Intelligence. In other words, both subject matters are intertwined and can be quite misconstrued for one another. Be that as it may, this book is all about Emotional Intelligence; thus, the focus will be given more to the concepts and definitions of that subject.

We can't fully delve into Emotional Intelligence without discussing emotions. Without these emotions, there would be no such thing as Emotional Intelligence. We need to have these emotions in order to make it possible for us to be able to measure and master them. There is no single person in the world without an iota of emotion in them. What differs is our level of indifference.

Meanwhile, the definition of emotion varies dependent on whoever is defining it. For example, an angry person might see emotions as the surge of innermost feelings which triggers certain hormones in the body as a result of outside circumstances. A calm person will tell you otherwise. Nevertheless, there are certain definitions which are quite accepted by all.

According to Sternberg, in his book, *In Search of the Human Mind*, "An emotion is a feeling comprising physiological and behavioral (and possibly cognitive) reactions to internal and external events."

In the same vein, Nairne posits that,

"An emotion is a complex psychological event that involves a mixture of reactions: (1) a physiological response (usually arousal), (2) an expressive reaction (distinctive facial expression, body posture, or vocalization), and (3) some kind of subjective experience (internal thoughts and feelings)."

Emotions are what we feel. They are independent and can hardly be controlled. For example, a temperamental individual would find it very difficult to control his or her anger no matter the number of hours spent in an anger management class. If the environment is not helping, then the classes would definitely have little or no effect on the individual.

Psychologically, emotions can be seen as a mental state where the mind translates our environment and outer circumstances into two possible outcomes – goodness or badness. Whichever outcome mind and body choose is exactly what we will feel. Let's take two quick examples, shall we? Our body responds to stimuli at the slightest touch. It's like our senses send a message to our brain, which in turn responds by making us feel the pain at the exact location of the touch.

If we get burnt by a fire while we are trying to drop a hot pot from the gas cooker, there would be a quick reflex between our hand and the pot. Thanks to stimuli, we would feel the pain exactly where we got burnt. That way, emotions of anger, pain, and probably sadness would set in as we would be left with a burnt hand.

In another example, a heartbroken person would definitely go berserk, becoming depressed and extremely sad. These are mostly the kinds of emotions that would rush in no matter how hard we try. With or without stimuli, these emotions are definitely going to show up. As James Averill rightly puts it,

"The concept of emotion . . . refer[s] to (1) emotional

syndromes, (2) emotional states, and (3) emotional reactions. An emotional syndrome is what we mean when we speak of anger, grief, fear, love and so on in the abstract. . . . For example, the syndrome of anger both describes and prescribes what a person may (or should) do when angry. An emotional state is a relatively short term, reversible (episodic) disposition to respond in a manner representative of the corresponding emotional syndrome. . . . Finally, and emotional reaction is the actual (and highly variable) set of responses manifested by an individual when in an emotional state: . . . facial expressions, physiological changes, overt behavior, and subjective experience."

Be that as it may, what really is Emotional Intelligence? Like Stoicism, Emotional Intelligence is the ability to express, master, and control emotions. If you possess this quality, then you are definitely a master of emotions. You will be able to know and identify your emotions before and after you feel them. That way, you will be able to manage your emotions effectively and efficiently.

With Emotional Intelligence, getting angry unnecessarily, feeling stressed out or even depressed would definitely not cross your path. Emotional Intelligence would not only help you manage your emotions well, but also allow you to relate well by mastering the emotions of the people around you. When our best friend tends to read our emotions like the back of their hand, as ignorant as we might be, we call it sheer luck. Don't get it twisted - that friend might have been able to master emotional intelligence, thereby, making it very easy for them to predict your emotions even before they occur.

Salovey and Mayer defined Emotional Intelligence as,

"The ability to monitor one's own and others' feelings and emotions, to discriminate among them, and to use this information to guide one's thinking and actions."

In the same vein, Emotional intelligence refers to the capability of a person to manage and control his or her emotions and possess the ability to control the emotions of others as well. In other words, they can influence the emotions of other people, also. When you can easily place your hands on the mood of the people around you; when you can show them what true and genuine relationship actually means; when you can predict their behavior by focusing on their emotions. Then, you can call yourself a master of Emotional Intelligence.

Emotional Intelligence is a very broad subject matter that comes with at least four different fields of study. These can also be known as concepts, terms, or areas as the case may be. These are as follows:

1. **Self- Awareness:** This is the first step toward mastering

your own Emotional Intelligence. This involves getting a grip of oneself as well as understanding our own emotions. When we are self-aware of our own feelings and emotions, then we are bound to make good choices as well as productive decisions.

Like true stoics, having control of our emotions would definitely shape us into a better man. I know you must be wondering how controlling your emotions would make you a better man. Yeah? Well, let's take Robbie for example.

Robbie is a 32-year-old doctor who works at a government renowned hospital. Before Robbie lost his wife, he was a very good doctor, probably the best the hospital had. He was fast with his hands, jovial with his patients, and nice to his co-workers. This is the real Robbie. Several months ago, he lost his wife to cancer, one of the deadliest diseases in the world today, and everything changed for Robbie.

Robbie blamed himself for not stopping what happened. He blamed himself for not being good enough. He blamed himself for everything. That way, he hit rock-bottom in his amazing career. Everything just went from bad to worse for him at home and work. He lost focus, he lost his confidence, and he lost his self-esteem. That is, until he came across the real meaning of Emotional Intelligence in a book he saw at a friend's place.

Robbie now understood how to control his emotions. He now understood that having self-control, self-awareness of your emotions, and self-esteem is the key to living a happy and fulfilled life. Like magic, his recovery was fast, smooth, and easy. Emotional Intelligence helped him dropped the guilt he had carried all by himself. Emotional Intelligence showed him light when he seems to have gotten lost. Emotional Intelligence shaped him into a better man.

This is the first step toward mastering your emotions. First, you need to accept them. Embrace them as they come. They are part of you - and as humans, we are definitely tied to them. If we get a call from a friend, we will definitely experience some emotions. If we are eating a plate of sweet pie, emotions will also come in. Even if it's just our morning walk, we will definitely feel emptions along the way. We are tied to it. We can't do without it. The best we can do is to acknowledge it, learn to live with it, and most of all, understand how to control it to our own advantage.

2. **Self-Control:** This is the second stage that comes after noticing and acknowledging our emotions. After accepting the realism revolving around our emotions, learning how to control it is the next best thing to do. Sometimes, when we feel pain in our body or heart, what normally happens next is the torrent of tears that will either wet our pillow or handkerchief. This is very

normal, especially for ladies.

Sometimes, it is very hard for us to be able to control how we feel. Feelings can be like a raging bull when they need to be. They can also be as calm as a dove, too. It all depends on the circumstances revolving around you. But when these feelings surge rapidly, there should be something you can do to bring the levels down again almost immediately.

Some people hum a song; others just let it out by shouting at no one in particular. Irrespective of how you bring down your levels, what should matter is how well the method works. Controlling your emotions perfectly is like a wildcard to success in your endeavors. Take this, for example, when you are in a competition with a fellow competitor, all both of you will think of is the cutthroat decisions, like finding the weakness or loophole of your competitor.

This is very normal. But, controlling your emotions without allowing them to cloud your judgment would give you an upper hand. If your competitor hits hard at your weak area, taking the hit with a smile on your face would definitely unbalance your competitor. He or she would feel confused and disorganized. Now, that is your secret weapon – controlling those emotions. Thus, when you strike back, your competitor would definitely not see that coming.

Having self-control would help give you a clear head each time the need arises. Even amidst turbulent storms in your mind, and raging emotions, you would still have the confidence and assurance that you are on the right path.

3. **Empathy:** This particular type of feeling comes after learning how to control your inner feelings and emotions. Not everyone has this particular kind of Emotional Intelligence. Showing empathy to anyone around you is the desired trait that can only be fully harnessed after knowing yourself. If you know what your feelings are, notice them, and even control them, then you will definitely be drawn toward others.

You would be able to consider the feelings of others. When you understand people's emotions and feelings, you are sure to know what their next move is. You will be able to predict their actions even before they carry them out. It is very normal for a teenage girl to cry over heartbreak. Obviously, it could be her very first relationship experience and this goes a long way is shaping most teenage girls you see out there.

Many teens just don't know how to hold all those feelings inside of them. This is why you would notice a heartbroken teenager becoming a shadow of herself. If you understand people's inner emotions, you will be able to draw conclusions about any heartbroken teenagers after interacting with them. You will be able to place what they need, what they probably hoped for, and how you can actually come into the scenario.

Reading people's emotions comes to some as a gift. Unlike the rigorous training, exercises, and training others go through in order to become a master of Emotional Intelligence, some just find it very easy. Be that as it may, when you understand the emotions of the people around you, you will be able to interact with them even better. You will be able to know when to stop and when to apply pressure.

That way, the relationship you are preserving would even grow stronger by the day. Daniel was a 40-year-old man who lost all his money and assets in a bad stock market transaction. At the age of 32, he had his life all set out for him. He had a sweet family, a house he could call his own, his dream car, and a fat account balance. But his world went from white to black the moment everything came crashing down.

On a fateful Thursday, he had set out to end it all. His family left him, he lost his house, he lost his car, and most importantly, he lost his sanity. What saved Daniel was Emotional Intelligence. He had met an Emotional Intelligence expert before going to end it all. This expert sensed the raging emotions bottled up inside of Daniel. He followed Daniel secretly and quickly alerted the relevant authorities when he was about to take his own life.

Now, this makes me wonder, what would have become of Daniel if he hadn't spoken to an Emotional Intelligence expert? What if Emotional Intelligence hadn't been in existence? What if there was no empathy to begin with? This showcases the importance of Emotional Intelligence in our lives.

4. **Social Skills:** Just like empathy, social skill deals with using our Emotional Intelligence power to influence people's lives – not for the worse, but for the better. Don't get it twisted, Emotional Intelligence has been abused and used for evil purposes by some miscreants. Though it deals with understanding oneself and the people around you, it never promises to change one's beliefs and character.

This is the most advanced stage on the verge of mastering Emotional Intelligence, when we can understand the emotions of others around us and use this understanding to exert an influence in the lives of these people. With social skills, you will be able to know how to relate with everyone and anyone, thereby, carrying everyone along.

Social skills are an aspect of Emotional Intelligence that deals with the relation of one's emotion with another person's emotion. That way, you can both influence each other one way or the other.

With Emotional Intelligence, our lives are bound to be far better than they would be without it. When we apply it, we are surely setting our path toward greatness. We are definitely making ourselves into a better version of what we were yesterday. So, instead of allowing our emotions to dictate and influence our way of thinking, we should take control of Emotional Intelligence. The next chapter will look into ways of identifying and improving Emotional Intelligence. You don't want to miss it.

Chapter Two

Identifying and Improving Emotional Intelligence in Yourself and in Others Around You.

When things start falling into place and people start liking us in our personal lives or at work, it's not because we are special or unique. It's also not because we are better than the rest. It's because we have been exploiting our Emotional Intelligence. Emotional Intelligence is what has made us amazing over these years. And the funny thing about it is that some of us don't even have the slightest idea about this subject matter.

If only they knew the importance of this particular trait; if only they know it had been their inborn Emotional Intelligence qualities that had been working well for them; if only they know people liked them not because of what they have but because of how well they relate to and understand them. Then they would really know the true importance of Emotional Intelligence.

From Self-awareness to Self-control, Empathy, and Social Skills, Emotional Intelligence goes deeper than you can fathom. Now, the question remains: how can one identify Emotional Intelligence in oneself or even within others? It is important to know that Emotional Intelligence varies in every individual. We all can't have the same Emotional Intelligence Quotient. It surpasses one another.

Where some people can use this Intelligence to manipulate and influence other people's decisions, others can only understand the emotions running through a second party. When Daniel Goleman published a book as regards this subject matter in 1995, most people in the world had been very ignorant of the concept.

As a psychologist and a journalist in the field of science, he had taken a liking to the series of topics surrounding emotions, feelings, and emotions. He had always believed that human beings have a tendency of holding and staying in control of their feelings and emotions. He relates his theory to lots of examples, thereby showcasing how emotions had to be the henchmen behind our failures in life.

According to him, if emotions can be checked properly, then success will be the only song man will hear as the chances of being successful will be on the rise. Ripple by ripple, his idea moved from place to place, thereby changing the way people think as regards behavioral patterns towards emotions. If emotions can be checked, our behavioral pattern will definitely change for the better.

Like true stoics believe, emotions make one weak. They

make one relax and chase nothing but failure and regression. When you are filled with emotions or allow your emotions to influence a very big part of your decision making, then you will find yourself making decisions that aren't even worth it. You will find yourself making compromises, all the days of your life.

So how do we really identify this Emotional Intelligence? How do we know we possess it? This is what this chapter will delve into. According to my own little understanding, I believe identifying Emotional Intelligence shouldn't be hard to pull off. To begin with, one needs to fully immerse himself with the subject matter and understand what the real meaning of Emotional Intelligence is. Now, here are the few points you should watch out for:

1. **Thinking About Feelings Almost All the Time:** This is probably one of the easiest ways to know and identify Emotional Intelligence in yourself. Like we pointed out in Chapter One of this book, the first stage to Emotional Intelligence is self-awareness, and this self-awareness deals with admitting to the fact that you have emotions running through you.

After this admission, a certain surge of emotions will start growing in you and you will now start having sober reflections. That way, we are bound to start thinking along with questions like: What are emotions? Why do we feel this way? Are they beneficial or detrimental? How can they influence my decisions for the better or worse?

These particular lines of thought will open up your mind to Emotional Intelligence. It will make you realize that Emotional Intelligence had been in you all along. What you should focus now on is how to really project this trait to the success of your everyday endeavors and that of everyone around you.

2. **When You Think Before You Act:** Many people in the world today lack this outstanding quality. This is why many of us end up making lots of regrettable decisions. Before we do anything, it's best if we first weigh the pros and cons of the decision.

That is the only way we can save ourselves from doing anything stupid or embarrassing ourselves in the long run. Its best we take a chill, sit back, and weigh our decisions before taking them. If you already possess this kind of amazing quality, then you are definitely intelligent emotionally without knowing it. This is also another way of identifying Emotional Intelligence in yourself or any other person.

3. **When You Strive Continuously to be the Master of Your Own Thoughts:** Even with the little or no experience you might have had as regard Emotional

Intelligence, if you find yourself trying hard to hold your emotions together, even in trying moments, then you obviously possess this amazing trait.

It is important to know that emotions can hardly be controlled. We can't possibly control how we feel no matter how hard we try. But what we can actually master is our outburst towards these emotions. What we can really be in control of is how we react to these series of emotions that we feel. If the circumstances around us get us easily irritated and, as a result cause anger and frustration in us, what we can do to manage these raging emotions is properly manage our outbursts.

That way, you will be in charge of yourself. Instead of being a slave to your emotions, you will be in control of them instead. That way, your life will definitely take good shape and strike a balance that would make you thrive. In the end, it will create harmony between your core values and your objectives.

4. **Learning from Your Mistakes and Criticism:** One thing that will help you identify Emotional Intelligence quickly in yourself or other people is the ability to pick up lessons from your mistakes and criticism. An ordinary person will normally feel bad when you criticize them heavily or lightly. Some might even give up totally after hitting a few stumbling blocks.

Someone with a high trait of Emotional Intelligence will not only thrive with criticisms but also ensure pick points from it. In fact, it is an avenue for self-development, self-reliance, and self-control. If these criticisms or mistakes don't get to you at all, then you are indeed intelligent emotionally. Instead of getting angry, you stay calm and learn from what was being said.

5. **Being Real at all Times:** When you say things as they should be without sugarcoating them, you are intelligent emotionally. And it is important to know that these kinds of realists have few friends. It's quite unfortunate that a lot of people in the world today don't want to take things as they are. They don't want to accept reality no matter how you interpret it for them.

Emotional Intelligence focuses on reality. When you take things as they are, you hold your core values dear to your heart, and you don't give in to emotions, then you are emotionally intelligent. Be that as it may, you need to be steadfast and real at all times. That is the only way you can beat your emotions.

6. **Having Empathy:** Empathy is one of the stages of Emotional Intelligence. When you possess this characteristic, then you are definitely good to go. What empathy does is to help you reconnect with the people around you. It will open up a pathway for a healthy

relationship between yourself and the people around you. When empathy sets in, all you think about is the welfare of the people around you. You will be able to help them by understanding their emotions first.

When I say empathy, I don't mean compromises. Sometimes, we tend to mix up the meaning of empathy. Empathy doesn't make us weak or meek. Instead, it makes us compassionate toward the feelings of others. Together, all of you can understand each other and build a much better and more meaningful relationship.

7. **Showing Appreciation and Acknowledgement:** Emotional Intelligence is all about selflessness and understanding. It's all about leading a better lifestyle and one of the ways to make this happen is via appreciation and acknowledgment. When you show this trait to the people around you, when you shower them with praises for any good work they've done, when you show them how much you believe in them, then you are bound to be trusted.

With appreciation and acknowledgment, you will inspire the people around you. And guess what? It doesn't even cost a dollar. If one holds this trait, then that person is definitely intelligent emotionally. Praises boost the morale of anybody. Make this your keyword and you will build strong relationships with the people around you in no time.

8. **Being a Good Advisor:** Only people that had mastered Emotional Intelligence can beat their chests to be good advisers. When you are completely free from the tricky hands of emotions, your words and decisions won't be influenced by them. Although being an emotional intelligence person will require you to be quite real with the people around you, the way and manner in which you present your words of advice should really matter.

In the verge of upholding your core values and principles, you can also be mild with your criticisms. When you present them well, it will only open up the hearts of people toward you. In other words, people will appreciate you more and even tell you more about themselves. When you see someone possess this attribute, then you know the rest.

9. **Being Apologetic When the Need Arises:** The goal of Emotional Intelligence is to make sure you don't lose connection with the people around you. Being emotionally intelligent doesn't mean you are superior to the rest. It just means you are capable of controlling your outbursts and you possess the power over your emotions. Therefore, you are not too big to be apologetic when the need arises.

What most people didn't realize is that saying "I'm sorry," will never make you weak. Instead, it will make you become a more mature person. This is what people with Emotional Intelligence understand perfectly well. If you are like this or know someone who doesn't find it hard to say those words, then you've found Emotional Intelligence.

10. **Forgiving and Forgetting:** Emotional Intelligence does not leave room for resentment or grudge. When you hold on to something that hurts, all you are doing is hurting yourself even more. It also means you are giving emotions a chance to lead you. When you hold on to something that hurts, it only means you aren't ready to move on. These emotions will definitely hold you down from progressing with your life.

But, when you forgive and forget, then you are giving yourself a chance to thrive. You are giving yourself a chance to see a new dawn. You are giving yourself a chance to see the light; a light that would lead to your peace of mind, prosperity, and plush.

Ways to Improve Emotional Intelligence

1. **Leave Your Comfort Zone:** We never can tell what will happen to us if we don't even try out something new. Sometimes, the best way to improve or move forward is to challenge oneself with a new set of measures. When you test new waters, you open yourself up for new exciting experiences. This can only happen when you

leave your comfort zone.

Emotions can be quite tricky. So when these emotions come, some people feel the best way to deal with these emotions is to avoid them. But, what is the assurance that these emotions will not come up again at a later date? Is this how we will be avoiding them when they come back? Why not look for a permanent solution by going outside your comfort zone.

Work toward a permanent solution. Face your fears if you have to. Make sure you hold yourself so as not to lose your way on the verge of finding a solution. No matter how shrewd it may look like, do not ignore your emotions. They may come back and bite you in the ass when you least expect it.

2. **Know Your Triggers:** Triggers are the factors that create a surge of emotions in us. Triggers can also be seen as conditions that create a tendency for us to feel emotional about certain circumstances. Thus, when you identify these triggers, your Emotional Intelligence will definitely improve for the better. You will know when and how to control your emotions even better.

When you know what your triggers are, you will be able to control the outbursts of your emotions. You would have been prepared beforehand before the emotions take you over. That way, your actions, decisions, and words will be controlled appropriately. When we have an idea of how our buttons work, only then will we be able to improve our Emotional Intelligence, if not entirely, at least to an extent.

In relation to outside forces, you will want to know why these outside forces become triggers and push your buttons. You will also want to know when they push your buttons. If noise is what irritates you, especially when you are trying to work, read, or even listen to something important, then you should adjust it.

3. **Not Making Decisions in a Bad Mood**: This is a very bad thing to do, especially when we make hasty decisions when we are angry or frustrated. These situations cannot be totally avoided. But, that doesn't mean we should fall into the trap. When we are in this bad mood, we should learn to be calm and collected.

After which we can make our decisions when we become sober. Someone who makes decisions out of anger or frustration will only be visited with one outcome, and that is regret. When we are in a bad mood and our emotions tend to get the better of us, we lose focus and sight of the good side that lingers.

When we are constantly living in a bad mood, when we start feeling irritated at every little thing that comes our way, either at work or at home, then it will be very helpful if we refrain from making decisions. Because these are decisions we might regret when we start becoming sober. So when we stop this act, we will definitely improve our Emotional Intelligence.

4. **Making Decisions in a Good Mood Should be Avoided, Too:** I know you might be surprised about this point, but believe me; you won't want to make decisions in a happy mood either. There is always a tendency for you to say or do things you aren't even capable of doing when you are extremely happy. Zed took his family to a football game on Saturday afternoon and luckily for him, they won the match in a grand style.

This made Zed very happy and he decided to take his children out on a treat to the only expensive resort available in the town. Unfortunately, he had very little in his pocket. What he has can't even take the kids to an average resort, let alone an expensive one. But, out of genuine happiness and thrill, he made a decision he can't really uphold.

Now, if you know this is the kind of person you are, then I would advise you to always keep your mouth shut each time you are happy. This would save you from getting yourself into more trouble or even embarrassing yourself in the long run. We should always learn to be conscious of our actions and deeds.

5. **Hold on to Your Core Values No Matter What:** Along the line, we tend to start out beautifully well with our newfound Emotional Intelligence. But, along the line, circumstances and events happening in our lives will continuously make us reach a breaking point. For example, the stress at work might be becoming too harsh, friends and family might become too demanding, and life as a whole may become quite challenging.

When you lose your values and principles, you tend to become a shadow of yourself. That is when we would advise you to start thinking back to when you found yourself. If we've lost that touch with our inner self, all we need to do is to reconnect with it. That is the only way we can rediscover ourselves. When we hit a setback, we should go back to our values and principles; they are the only cushion we can fall back on.

That makes it a wrap with the various ways of identifying and improving your Emotional Intelligence. All you need to do is to look inward and find these outstanding qualities in yourself. Believe me - we all have these qualities in us, at least some, if not all. If only we can learn to make good use of them, our Emotional Intelligence will improve beyond measure.

Chapter Three

Secrets to Boosting Your Spirituality and Tapping into an Endless Amount of Joy

Spirituality comes with an open mind. It comes with a mind that is devoid of emotions, feelings, and unstable conditions. In the course of our lives, there are certain occasions where things seem to be going south, where everything and anything we engage ourselves in end up being unsuccessful, where our most cherished relationships end up getting sour as we lose that connection with our friends and family.

In the same vein, we may be forced to withdraw into our shell. We may be forced to be a shadow of ourselves. Instead of being the ever-smiling and carefree lady or gentleman many had known us to be, we start becoming something different simply because we've lost that touch with happiness and joy in our lives. Now, this is where Emotional Intelligence comes in as a way of boosting your spirituality into reaching your inner self. That way, you will become a better version of yourself in no time.

Racheal had been a straight-A student right from her pre-college days. Racheal would even go on to tutor many of her colleagues because she was that good. Many referred to her as the female Albert Einstein of their time. This academic prowess brought lots of joy and happiness into the lives of Racheal and her family. But everything turned when she lost her dad after taking her final exams. She lost the focus and the joy she derived from being an academician.

Her dad was her inspiration and support. The moment her dad died, she felt the need to quit. Not until she came across this the concept of Emotional Intelligence as a method of boosting one's spirituality. There and then, she knew all she needed to do was to find herself, again. She knew all she needed to do us to go back and meditate until she opened her inner chakras. That was the only way she could be free from any form of anger, sadness, guilt, and regret. And it worked like magic. She got into college and has been acing her exams ever since.

Now, when I say spirituality, I'm not talking about the voodoo kind of spirituality, in case your mind starts wandering toward that direction. Instead, I'm talking about following a pathway which will lead to a better version of what you were yesterday. It is important to know that achieving this feat doesn't come easy at all. In fact, you will need to put much work, dedication, and commitment into it for it to work. You will really need to let go of the things that are tying you down.

For example, you can't suddenly want to start meditating with a heavy heart. You and I know that is not possible. For meditation to work effectively and efficiently, your heart needs to be free. You will really need to drop any connection or attachment you have with the world. That is the only way you can reach your inner self. This is where Emotional Intelligence comes in. If Emotional Intelligence teaches you to control your outbursts and keep a check on your emotions, don't you think your spirituality level is going to increase? Don't you think you will be able to find yourself and at the same time connect with the people around you even better?

There are lots of benefits attached to Emotional Intelligence. All you need to do is just open your eyes to the possibilities around you. When you have an improved relationship with your co-workers at your place of work, you will thrive at your place of work with many people watching after you. When you have a good connection with the people at home, it means you have people to fall back to and that would result in joy and happiness.

And if ever you start getting a surge of emotions that would be too much for you to handle, the best thing to do is to stay calm at that particular moment. If possible, meditate for a while. This will really calm your emotions. But, if you lost your values and principles along the line as the emotions may seem to have taken over, spirituality will help you regain the lost balance and stability in your life. It will help you see past those emotions, no matter how shrouded they might be.

Kane, who was supposed to be promoted to the position of a Junior Partner in his law firm, woke up one morning with joy and happiness in his heart. He knew this was definitely going to be his promotion. He knew this was definitely his day and he was well prepared for it. He had gotten the right tuxedo, the right shoes, and the right tie. But unfortunately for him, Emily was given the promotion instead. You can imagine the hurt on Kane's face as he felt his world crumble right in his presence.

This stunt affected Kane a lot and made him sad all throughout the week. Like a snail, he regressed back into his shell. He lost his cheerfulness, his joy, and his charisma along the line. But with spirituality, he gradually found his way back to being happy and ecstatic. It wasn't an easy journey for him, but in the end, he was able to found his way back. This was only possible because he was able to let go of his covetousness and his attachments to this world, and control of his outburst.

Now, you can be like Racheal and Kane. You can control your emotions and manage them effectively with spirituality. When you feel lost and sad, you should always remember that there is a pathway which you can follow to reach happiness and immense joy. That pathway is spirituality. Ripple by ripple, you will find yourself growing and building a stronger connection with your inner self. Your values and principles would now be your guiding angels.

Additionally, it is important to know that we can try lots of techniques and ways toward reaching our inner selves. Whichever one that works for us should be our own special technique. You shouldn't copy others by following their ways. What if their ways don't even work for you? Also, you should know that what has worked for you over the years might now work for you again. So, it is vital for you to be highly flexible towards reaching your inner self.

You can also try out any old forms of spirituality that you can think of, no matter how traditional they may seem. What should matter is how effective and efficient they seem. If it helps you concentrate and foster your journey to the other realm, then I would advise you to keep doing it. Achieving growth, stability, and balance in one's life is not a small thing to do. In fact, it can be quite tricky at times. One minute, you might be making progress and the next, you will just realize how stuck you had been. This is where versatility comes in.

Now, what will this chapter do? This chapter will enlighten you on the connection between spirituality and Emotional Intelligence. It will delve into the working relationship between both subject matters. If in the end, you still can't find the answers you are looking for, then we would advise you to stick with us through the remaining chapters. This book will definitely hold answers to your overall questions and mysteries.

Your spirituality journey is your own. Whatever you do to make it amazing is really up to you. When you start feeling pains, hurt, sadness, and even regret, what you need to do is to start going spiritual. If ever everyone rejects you, your inner self is always there to embrace you and show you your true self. Go back to it and make peace with yourself. It is only after making peace with yourself that you can make peace with the rest of the world. So, how do you strengthen your spirituality, I'll tell you.

1. **Forgiveness:** There is no better way to achieve ultimate peace. When you forgive, you are letting go of the heavy load on your head. When you forgive, your heart becomes lighter. This is the first step towards making a change in our lives. With lots of bad things that are taking place in this part of the universe, there is only a little or no chance at all that we might end up hurting someone or being hurt by someone either intentionally or even unintentionally.

Whichever way the case may be, we shouldn't hold on to such a negative feeling. Trust me; it does no good at all to hold a grudge against someone for a long time. Whether we like it or not, a grudge will only harden our hearts and make us look extremely bad in front of others. In the end, we will not even be able to concentrate fully at work, at home or with friends. That way, our connections with friends and families will end up getting strained. This is not what we want for ourselves.

Spiritually, a hardened heart cannot connect with his or her inner self. This is a vital rule that guides all spiritual levels. You need to be sure that your heart is completely free from hate and grudges in order for you to connect with your other side. Thus, we would advise you to practice forgiveness every blessed day of your life. Seek out those who have trespassed against you. Forgive them even if they don't act like they need forgiveness. This will only save you additional stress.

2. **Honesty in Words and Deeds:** One thing we shouldn't forget is that an honest heart has nothing to hide. When we are honest with our friends and family, no matter the circumstances, we are opening a path to a stronger connection. When our heart is free from lies and dishonesty, our spirituality level automatically rises. Thus, when you are honest in words and deeds, you will never lose that connection with your true self.

Accept your flaws and shortcomings. If you are wrong,

admit it to others. If you err against anybody, go and apologize to them. Always keep an honest relationship. When we start shading our dealings from our friends and families, suspicion starts to arise. That way, there will be no connection at all and the little we have preserved will eventually fade away. If we start learning the true meaning of honesty, we will realize that telling another your deepest fear, your inner secret, and your flaws won't make you little.

Instead, it will show how much they can trust and believe in you. It will only tell them the extent to which they can connect with you. So, go out with your friends, invite them over for dinner if possible, and let go of every standard you have set for yourself. Expectations and standards will only make you become too stiff and stagnant.

You can even organize a support group. If you don't have the means to organize one, then you can simply attend one with family and friends. In case you start feeling shy, there are many support groups where your identity is not even required. Feel free to join. You will realize that support groups can be very helpful, too. You can also get attached to a spiritual leader. Make him/her your role model. They will gladly show you the path to follow in terms of honesty. Spiritual leaders always have a tendency to listen. Don't hesitate to pour out the hurt.

3. **Reach Your True Self:** We alone know ourselves and we

are each unique in our own way. When we start feeling bad or drifting off from our purpose in life, there is a need for us to come back to shape and one of the best ways to do that is to explore our inner self. When we explore our inner selves, we are reaching out to the real parts of us that had stayed locked inside of us, the real side of us that completes us.

When we are true to ourselves, we are creating a life of plush, peace, and stability for ourselves. When we explore our real selves, we are directly or indirectly boosting our spirituality. That way, only immense joy, and happiness will await us at the end of our journey. Now, how do you explore your inner self? It's pretty simple.

To begin with, you can start by writing down important moments in your life. Write about the challenges you've faced and how well you overcame them. If you do this well, you will be able to use this writing as your guiding points and principles in your future endeavors. You can also be mentored by a spiritual leader. They would be able to fill you in as regards your self-exploration. You can also follow the path of meditation. This can only work with enough focus. In the end, you will be able to reach your true potential spirituality.

4. **Value Your Principles:** At the end of it all, our principles and core values are all we've got. They are the guidelines

that we should follow in order to reach the peak of our spiritual growth. Our principles should be our knight in shining armor. They should hold our thoughts together and make us focus on what we really need to do. Make your principles your rules, and life would fall into place. However, there are circumstances that may warrant us to skip these principles.

When this happens, you don't have to beat yourself up too much about it. It's true our principles are the lights that shine our pathway to balance and stability. But, it is not true that skipping the principles once will make us lose our connection. Principles should be flexible. They should be able to fit into the current situation of things. That way, we will be able to adjust ourselves easily when the need arises.

5. **Understanding Spirituality Itself:** Spirituality itself is a very broad topic. We need to first understand what it really means before we can decide to delve into it. With lots of people making up misconceptions about the subject matter, we would advise you to find a well-accepted definition and meaning. That way, you can be able to interpret spirituality in your own terms.

So, what do you need to do after understanding the concept of Spirituality in your own terms? It's pretty simple. We would advise you to reflect on it. Think deeply about how spirituality can take you to exactly where you want to be. Think of how it would help you boost your level of spirituality. If you want, you can write them down, too. When you really understand something properly, you will be able to tweak it to your own preference.

6. **Your Body is Your Temple; Take Care of It:** The body is the vessel that holds the mind and the soul. Without a perfect and well-conditioned body, there would be no spirituality. It is important to know that both the body and the mind are connected in the sense that one can't function aside from the other. In other words, always take good care of your body. That is a way of boosting your spiritual levels.

So, the question now remains, how can we really care for our body in order to maintain a healthy lifestyle? First and foremost, you need to eat well. A balanced diet should always be maintained in order to support a healthy body. Secondly, sleeping well is also very important. When you don't sleep well, your body will definitely not feel right. Then lastly, you need to exercise occasionally. Then you exercise the body and keep fit, you are only inviting a healthy body. If your body is sound, then reaching the peak of your spirituality shouldn't be hard to pull off.

Thus, you need to find out which one works well for you. What works for your friends might not work for you. This is why you need to figure out what your preferences are. Stick to those preferences and your body will be just fine.

7. **Relate with People of Like Minds:** When you move with people who are far higher than you spiritually or people that will always like to scale higher in terms of their spirituality, then there is a very high chance of you improving your level of spirituality. If you are always with people like this, it will be easy for you to connect with them spiritually. Aside from these connections, it will also be very easy for you to seek out corrections and new ideas on how to approach or boost your Spirituality.

Together, you can reach out to more people, thereby connecting with even more people than you had earlier imagined. You can form a group or even join one to be with these people. You can share ideas, argue out assumptions, and reach a necessary agreement if the need arises. There is always an advantage to that particular kind of group. Imagine the positive vibes you will feel when the group connects spiritually.

Well, there you have it. It's no longer a secret. These are exactly the same secrets lots of these so-called masters of Emotional Intelligence won't tell you. Immerse yourself in it, devote yourself to it, and make sure you follow it to the letter. The rest will play itself out. The next chapter promises to be more exciting and entertaining - trust me.

Chapter Four

Proven Emotional Intelligence Strategies to Drive Your Success, Power, and Motivation

In life, we all have to subscribe to different strategies if we truly want to lead a life we can be proud of. These strategies can be long cuts or short cuts. They can be negative or positive. They can be anything at all. But one function they all perform perfectly is to make sure we reach our goals or objectives. If you are a stockholder, there are strategies which you have to employ in order not to lose out in the stock market. If you are an entrepreneur, there are also cutthroat strategies you need to make use of in order to stay at the top of your game.

Be that as it may, you can't reach a milestone in life cutting out strategies to use. These strategies will serve as the guiding principles toward achieving that goal in life. Now, as regards Emotional Intelligence, what are these strategies that would ensure your Emotional Intelligence continues to improve day in and day out? What strategies are there to employ for you to be able to reach the peak of your Emotional Intelligence? What strategies would you employ in order to achieve remarkable levels of motivation, success in your career, and the immense power of your emotions?

To begin with, many people have found it quite unnecessary to engage themselves in these strategies. This is because technology today has evolved to the extent where intelligence can be tested in no time. The IQ quiz can explain our level of intelligence in no time. That way, if a person whose IQ is quite high took the test, he or she might be subjected to start thinking testing the Emotional Intelligence would be quite unnecessary. After all, their IQ is very high, thus, their Emotional Intelligence should also be high.

Now, this is a very wrong notion. You can have a very high IQ but end up with a very low Emotional Intelligence. The ability to think fast differs from the ability to control emotions. They are two different things entirely. According to some group of scholars, they see Emotional Intelligence as the, "capacity to be aware of, control, and express one's emotions, and to handle interpersonal relationships judiciously and empathetically."

Now, do you still think Emotional Intelligence is irrelevant? Do you think your IQ alone would make you a better person? If your mentality has changed, then welcome to the world of Emotional Intelligence. But, if you are still thinking in the same line, then I would recommend you follow the next chapters. That way, you will definitely find the answers you seek. Be that as it may, it is important to know that we live in a world of interactions - or should I call it globalization.

We live in a world where interactions become a must for us as individuals living under the same cosmos. So, how would you maintain these relationships and connections if you don't even know the real meaning of relationships and connections? This is exactly what Emotional Intelligence would add to your horizon. It would show you the possibilities around you, thereby fostering your relationships and connections as well as helping you reach your inner self.

Trust me; you can only reach your true potential when you know yourself. When you immerse yourself with the idea of who you truly are, that is the only time which you will be able to move forward. In the end, you will feel inspired by every day setting out easy and perfect. That is the only time where you will get motivated, inspired, and achieve ultimate success.

Over the years, Emotional Intelligence has been gaining momentum, with top companies of the world adding the concept to the list of important values and virtues they need before employing new hires. With time, it has moved from the personal skill people use to reach their inner self, build, and maintain relationships to professional skills people seek out before making a hire. If you are wondering what Emotional Intelligence has to do with being professional, then allow me to break it down for you.

As an important skill in professionalism, Emotional Intelligence will allow the workers to remain professional no matter the circumstances they find themselves in. If we can master our own feelings and emotions at work, we will be able to keep everything professional. We have heard of cases where employees make out at work or even after work. This unprofessional act may come to bite the firm deep in the ass if fast measures aren't taken. But, with Emotional Intelligence, the tendency for that particular kind of stunt to happen would be close to zero.

These raging feelings would be kept in check and any form of the unprofessional act would be discouraged entirely. Emotional Intelligence would further encourage empathy for others around you, self-awareness for your own emotions and feelings, and the right motivation that would enable you to keep a straight head at work or at home. To cut it short, Emotional Intelligence leads to professional alertness and efficiency. It would also open up our mind to the performance of our friends and family.

So what is this chapter all about? This chapter will familiarize you with these well-known and well-trusted strategies of Emotional Intelligence to open up a new pathway for motivation, success, and immense control over your emotions. Now, what are these strategies? There is only one way to find out, yeah?

1. **Trusting Your Intuitive at all Times:** One thing we should never take for granted is our intuition or "gut." According to popular research carried out many years ago, it was agreed that our intuition is a signal or warning our true self sends to us when the need arises - and they are hardly wrong. You should know that your gut is an effective and efficient tool that should be used to your advantage adequately. Do not neglect it for no just reason.

To all rational thinkers, intuition is a very important part of their decision-making process. They never joke with what their gut tells them. If harnessed properly, this can be a very important tool for you to achieve complete success, power, and motivation in your life. Be that rational thinker. Always trust your intuition. When you start feeling odd about a particular person or project, do the needful. Take the necessary step so as not to end up with regrets.

That way, we would only end up making better decisions about our lives, using sound judgments about our professionalism, and improving our Emotional Intelligence. You will come to realize that you were missing out when you did not trust your intuition.

2. **Quiet the Mind if You Can:** Now in cases of too much

brouhaha, this strategy can come in handy for you if you know how to use it. And if you don't, I would suggest you learn it. Learn to shut everything out of your mind. And when I refer to everything, I'm talking about the noises, the stress, the arguments, and so much more that would hinder you from concentration. If you cannot manage it, then just shut it out.

That is the only way you will be able to think properly and accurately. Most people end up losing focus when they are stressed, tensed, and in a situation where noises are just too much. There is no way you would be able to think rationally or even communicate clearly in this state. Thus, if you don't have the ability to shut everything out, then we would advise you to walk away from that place. That is the only way you would be able to think properly.

But if you can clear your mind even amidst the stress around you, then that is just perfect. This strategy would come in handy because it would help you accelerate your rate of thinking rationally. You can easily slip into meditation during that time. It would help you keep the focus on what to do. In the end, your Emotional Intelligence would improve greatly, and this improvement would lead to motivation and success.

3. **Know that you are Different from Your Emotions:** This is the first step to greatness. The moment you establish

the fact that you are not your emotions, you will move forward. That is when you will realize that nothing can stop you from realizing your dreams. When we start having the notion that our emotions lord over us, that is when we have finally accepted defeat.

Don't get it twisted; feeling the streams of emotions running through us is what makes us human. Just because you don't want your emotions to lord over you doesn't mean you should start forcing yourself on not feeling anything for. Even if that is possible, it is not right. Feelings and emotions are natural circumstances we cannot stop. We can only control the way we react. Thus, instead of depriving yourself these emotions, you should concentrate on controlling how you react. Then, start by knowing your emotions don't make you who you are. You are not your emotions.

4. **Be Optimistic at all Times:** This is one of the strongest tools that you can use to achieve motivation, success, and power. Optimism comes with a clear mind. A troubled mind cannot be optimistic as their hopes will be shrouded by fear, uncertainty, and frustration. As someone who is emotionally intelligent, you should be optimistic. That way, you would be able to place optimism in the right situations and circumstances.

But before you do that, ask yourselves these questions: Are you the kind of person who just sees things as they should be or believes there is more to it than meets the eye? Are you the type of person that doesn't see things differently from being a combination of 100% sheer luck and 0% practice? Are you the type of person that believes things happen as they should, thus leaving no room for blame? If you are, then you really need to practice being optimistic more often. When you are optimistic, it inspires and motivates you to reach great success.

5. **Your Ego is Your Downfall; Kill It:** Ego is the number one enemy to man right from the inception. Our ego had always been the cankerworm that eats our whole being. It stretches out to how we react to the situations and circumstances around us. It takes over our decision making. In fact, it is present in every step of our lives. Now, the best way to reach our peak is to forgo our ego. When we let go of our ego, we will be shocked at how things would play out differently than we had earlier anticipated.

It is important to know that no one can make you feel inferior or awful about yourself if you don't give them the power to. If you let yourself feel less than what you are, that is the only way they can make you look inferior. According to a study on ego, it was concluded that ego is the beginning of every downfall. If our ego is in the way of our success, we would definitely not make progress.

Additionally, there is no place for ego in Emotional Intelligence. As a matter of fact, you can't be filled with ego and at the same time claim to be a master of Emotional Intelligence. When you are filled with ego, your inner self stays far away from you. There will be no connection at all so long you still harbor ego in your heart. So start by killing off your ego. Happiness and success will definitely follow suit.

6. **Embrace Your Emotions:** This strategy also works perfectly. Understanding your emotions perfectly is one of the tenets of Emotional Intelligence. But, acknowledging them as they come would definitely improve your Emotional Intelligence, thereby fostering motivation, success, and power to control the outcome of your emotions. Unlike many people that would prefer to just neglect or even look the other way when these emotions come, accepting and acknowledging them is the best way to do it.

When you accept, understand, and at the same time acknowledge these emotions, you are definitely going to find emotions that are going to be of good use. Don't get it twisted; these emotions can come in two ways, good or bad. But what should matter is our ability to use and manipulate them for the better. If we can understand our emotions properly, we will be able to use them for our own good. There and then, motivation will set in, paving the way for success.

7. **Think Before You Speak:** Sometimes, our emotions end up carrying us away so much that we end up not knowing exactly what we have just spewed out from our mouths. For example, when certain expectations aren't met, we tend to start feeling frustrated and tensed, thereby, using our mouths to say things we don't even mean. The reason we make these mistakes is that we hardly think before we talk or act in cases like these.

Additionally, when these expectations are met beyond our imagination, we tend to start feeling ecstatic and extremely happy, thereby, ending up saying things we can't even do. This is very common when people end up getting what they want or even achieving success in their endeavors. If only we can think before we speak even in the happiest and saddest moments, then we would realize that everything won't look so complicated in the long run.

Let's find a way to conceal our emotions. And if we cannot do that, then let's make sure we don't utter a word all through the phase. Our words are the true reflection of our hearts. We should learn how and when to use them appropriately. Now, how do you maintain this? It's simple. You can get attached to someone you can trust. That way, you can let out anything you have in you before you end up exploding. Afterward, you will feel light. We end up making these mistakes with our words because of the baggage we carry.

8. **Imagine yourself to be Someone Else:** Instead of judging others from afar, how about you go close to them or, better still, try wearing their shoes to see where it pinches? According to a popular saying, "What turns out to be a 6 to you might be a 9 to me." This doesn't mean we are both wrong. Instead, it's just our perspective that differs."

Instead of seeing ourselves as perfect, how about we try seeing things from others' perspectives? If we start thinking that our thoughts, decisions, and opinions are always right, then there will be no room for development and improvement at all. We will be stuck in our own world without even realizing it. Let's try and give others a chance to explain their own opinions. Let's hear them out too and observe their points. You may be shocked at how wrong you have been all along.

Be that as it may, whenever you try to boss over anybody or impose your decisions on them, take a few minutes to hear them out. Listen to their perspectives. Try and put yourself in their situation so as to have a deep understanding of their notion. This is the only way to foster a healthy relationship with the people around you. When you always try to listen to yourself all the time, your connection with them gets severed and strained.

9. **Law of Attraction:** There is no better way to achieve complete motivation and success than to believe in the law of attraction. When you believe that what comes around actually goes back around, then there is nothing stopping you from desisting from doing negative things to the people around you. Remember, what you reap is what you sow. Thus, wouldn't you rather sow goodness?

When you think of only good, then success will definitely come knocking at your door. When you think better, happiness will also become part of you. That way, your journey to the other side of you will always be smooth and easy. Believe it or not, karma is real. And when it comes knocking, you won't even expect it. This is why you should always treat people right no matter what the circumstances.

10. **Always Give Others a Listening Ears:** According to Mahatma Gandhi, we should, "speak only if it improves upon the silence."

These few words should be coated in gold as they hold great meaning. When you are a good listener, you are definitely making it easy for the other person to feel free in continuing his or her conversation. Quality listening gives the other person confidence in what he or she is saying. Even if what the person is saying doesn't add up, allow them to finish making their point before you interrupt. Stopping a person halfway in a conversation doesn't really go down well with some people.

Thus, give the listening ear to anyone that needs it. It's another way of fostering your relationships with the people around you via Emotional Intelligence. In the end, you will be able to derive motivation from the things you've heard, the things you've been able to digest, and the things you feel would be useful later.

There you have it. Do you want to succeed so badly in your endeavors, but have been faced with so much defeat, you're about to give up? Do you need motivation as regards your business or relationships? All you need to do is to follow the tips I'd listed above. Trust me - everything will change for the better in no time.

Chapter Five

How You Can Boost Your Emotional Intelligence Almost Overnight

In the previous chapter, we looked into the effective and efficient strategies one can use to boost Emotional Intelligence and also to reach a good level of motivation and success in life. In as much as Emotional Intelligence is concerned, you cannot lead a good life without a touch of it. Either intentionally or unintentionally, you just have to exude true Emotional Intelligence in order for you to be truly happy in the end.

As a trending topic in the United States of America, there has been a call for the introduction and development of this subject matter in the society at large. The government now believes Emotional Intelligence is the backbone to leading a happy life and a happy individual life equates to a happy society. If the people of a particular region or geographical location are happy, there will be little or no hindrance to the policies of the government. That way, the government can achieve its policies and the people will also remain happy.

No matter how you look at it, Emotional Intelligence provides a win-win situation. If you are a master of

Emotional Intelligence, very little will get to you; that is, if they get to you at all. You will be in control of your tempos and your push button would definitely be in your own hands. Where your intellectual ability gives you the avenue by which your thinking rate would be very fast, Emotional Intelligence provides you with an avenue where your levels of emotional outburst, relationships, connections, and spirituality remains at their best.

Be that as it may, a lot of people have asked quite a whole lot of vital questions about Emotional Intelligence over the past few years since it became a trend in the American society. As a novice or beginner to the world of Emotional Intelligence, it is very normal for you to start acting funny and all worked up over nothing. Even the Stoics still finds it hard to manage and keep their emotions in check, let alone a normal person with no philosophy at all.

Thus, don't push yourself. Feel free to ask those that are more knowledgeable than to you in this line of discussion. Remember, he who asks never loses his way. You can ask how much time it will take for one to be a complete master of their emotions. You can also ask when one can actually master the control of their emotions. You can equally ask if someone can build up this outstanding trait overnight. Feel free to test all boundaries. It's better to know what you are about to enter before even making a move.

Now, if you are seeking answers revolving around Emotional Intelligence, then this book is the right book for you. But if your questions are revolving around gaining this Emotional Intelligence trait overnight, then this chapter is a must read for you. Moussa, who was an immigrant from Syria due to the war that had ravaged his home, came into the United States of America with the hope of starting afresh, with the hope of getting greener pastures.

As a Muslim and an Arab, the society didn't actually welcome him with open arms. Every day that passed, he was treated with disdain and discrimination. Quite a lot of people in America hold the view that these immigrants are nothing but miscreants who have come to take up jobs meant for the real Americans, thus the cold treatment Moussa received from the people around him. No matter how hard he tried to make friends, they just weren't into him.

His Middle-East accent and religious background gave him up no matter how hard he tried to blend in. But the big question Moussa had to answer was if he truly needed to change his true self in order to get a pass into society. It took Moussa a while to accept himself and the way in which the system works. When Moussa began making peace with himself and accepting himself just the way he was, that is when the society started smiling him.

He had wanted to blend in so bad, but nothing worked.

Then he discovered the emotionally intelligent part of him. He realized the only way for him to be free from these awful treatments he had been receiving was for him to connect with his inner self. Nevertheless, when you also understand the emotions of people around you, you can use them to your own benefit. You can harness those feelings and use them as your shield when the need arises.

Additionally, you will also need a very big chunk of Emotional Intelligence in order to succeed at work or in your professional life. You will need it to relate with others in school. You will also need Emotional Intelligence in your career path in order to be successful. This is how important Emotional Intelligence can be. I bet you can now see the reason why some people want to learn this outstanding trait overnight. The question one should ask him or herself now is if it is possible to exude this outstanding trait in one day.

Imagine waking up one morning with an emotionless feeling? Can you picture yourself in that state? Don't get it twisted; I'm not implying that being expressionless is an awful state to be. In fact, it is an outstanding trait that can only be mastered by the disciplined. But just picture yourself waking up like that without going through any form of training at all, without putting in much effort, and without working towards that goal. Do you think that is possible?

If you are of the thought that such cannot happen

overnight, then I would say you are right. If you are also thinking in the direction of believing such a thing can happen in one day, then I won't rule your assertions wrong either. It is important to know that everybody has his or her own limit. Aside from that, there are forces which can push us to be what we don't even expect to be. There are forces that can change us totally from the inside in a single swoop without even recognizing the change at first.

This is what may happen to you when you become emotionally intelligent overnight. First, you must have had or possessed such outstanding trait as we outlined in Chapter Two of this book. You must have been identified with lots of characteristics and traits pointing towards one thing – Emotional Intelligence. For example, you must have been caring towards others, you must have been empathetic towards the emotions of your friends and family, you must have been able to understand your own emotions, and you must have been able to give listening ears and great advice when the need arises. These are just a few of the characters you must have exuded before growing your Emotional Intelligence overnight.

Secondly, you must have been having the notion of becoming a master of your feelings. It is important to know that things just don't happen without our consent or desire for them to happen. For you to develop this outstanding trait overnight, then you must have first desired for it to happen. You must have wished for the power to control your emotions. That would open up a whole new channel in you for the development of this trait. Desiring something means your whole body and mind wants it, thus making sure they are both prepared for the reception of what you desire. That way, you won't have a problem trying to adjust yourself.

When we prepare our mind toward becoming a master of our emotions, we are definitely making sure everything is intact. Desiring the outstanding trait is one thing, but preparing your mind is another different thing entirely. Prepare yourself adequately because Emotional Intelligence can come with a lot of perseverance and patience. Now, the question is, how patient are you? Can you really look the other way in a stressed and tensed situation? If you can't do this, then how do you plan on mastering your emotions? Thus, desire the trait, and then prepare yourself.

Thirdly, you should also learn to know what to do at the right time. This is a very important characteristics only true Stoics and masters of Emotional Intelligence can wield as many times as they like. Knowing how to act in certain circumstances or situations will definitely build you up emotionally in no time. When you comport yourself well even in times of crisis, when you stay calm even during turmoil, when you smile even during disturbances, it's not because you don't have feelings or emotions running through you, but because reacting negatively won't solve anything, and you know this better than anyone.

Instead, you chose to remain calm and collected. You chose to think about damage control instead of going crazy over the whole situation. The funny part of every tensed situation is that when you stay calm and look deep into it, you will realize that the solution and panacea had been right there staring at you. All you needed to do was to think fast and stop allowing your emotions to take the better part of you. This is how confusing emotions can be. This is why many great men of today point at emotions as the number one killer of ideas and dreams.

When you start putting your emotions first, you will achieve very little in life. Believe it or not, putting your emotions first without doing the right thing at the right time will spoil a whole lot of things for you. It will damage the relationships you have toiled to build for years with family and friends. At work, you will have a strained relationship with your co-workers, which can be very bad for you no matter how you interpret that. Things will just stand still in your life with no one ready to connect with you except your ego. Therefore, always do the right thing at the right time.

Fourthly, you should learn to keep the cup of your spirituality flowing no matter what. It is important to know that when others neglect you or turn their back against you totally, only one thing will remain – your inner self. This is the part of you that can never leave you but can definitely neglect you. It all depends on how strong your spirituality levels are.

In case you don't know, our Spirituality level can hasten up the improvement of our Emotional Intelligence and vice versa. If you say both Emotional Intelligence and Spirituality are two sides to a coin, then you are not entirely wrong. No matter what you do, don't allow it to affect your Spirituality because it would always come in handy when the need arises. And when you have your Spirituality levels intact, then I don't see anything that would stop you in getting your Emotional Intelligence level back up in one night.

Be that as it may, you should try a whole lot of meditation whenever you feel stressed or tensed about a situation. If you feel the situation is going to take a very big chunk of your emotions, then start meditating in your mind. This will help you stay calm and vanish the emotions that had been building up inside of you. All thanks to technology, you can also try out lots of apps which can help you reshuffle your emotions if the need arises.

Additionally, having someone to look up to can also come in handy when the need arises. Trust me; sometimes it can be very hard to maintain the same level of Spirituality over a long period of time all by yourself. This is where you need a spiritual coach, a real-life spiritual mentor, a well-known spiritual leader, or even a spiritual role model. That way, you would have someone to keep you on your toes, someone who's spiritual life is worthy of emulation, someone who will be ready to listen to your woes and drag you back up whenever you fall.

Fifthly, always keep a to-do list, every blessed day of your life. As a beginner, this is the first thing I'm going to tell you if you come to me with the problem of not being able to discover the emotionally intelligent side of you. I would tell you to go back home and make a list of the things you would want to do today and the day after that until infinity. It is very normal for beginners of Emotional Intelligence to slip up and allow their emotions to take control over them in certain situations, especially when they have tried hard to dodge the situation. Some might even forget Emotional Intelligence exists for a while and act on without caution.

This is why I would recommend a to-do list being a novice. Go home, make your list. Point out the crazy scenes from the past and how you reacted to the situation. Then point out areas where you need to brush off and the ones you would need to adjust totally. This is a very good start. After making your list, then see how things go from there. You will be shocked at how well you will respond to any situation that comes knocking.

Now, that is not all. I always make sure I tell those beginners the truth of Emotional Intelligence. It is important to know that even the masters of this trait didn't get it right in one swing. So, there are going to be one or two glitches on your first few days. If at all such things may occur, then write them down also. Learn from them. We are all improving every day. Ripple by ripple, you will also get there. And if your friends and family start noticing any change in you, then you should know that Emotional Intelligence is taking your life to a whole new level.

Sixthly, set your principles and values before starting out. It is important to know that nothing can be achieved in a year, not to mention overnight without setting the foundation; core values and principles. These values and principles would serve as the base of every idea, notion, tenet, character, and so much more. That way, when everything ends up falling apart or going south, the one thing that will remain is your values. They will set the pace for you to follow.

Thus, if you don't have a value or principle that would guide you all through this journey until you become a master yourself, then I would strongly recommend you get one for yourself. How would you find your way back to yourself when your emotions have already taken you over completely? How would you find the right path to follow as regards Emotional Intelligence if you didn't have your values and principles to guide you through it? You can't just wake up one morning with the idea of becoming a master of Emotional Intelligence. Something must have driven the idea out of you. Something must have grown the seeds in you.

Now, that something is your value; don't lose it. Don't get carried away along the line, forgetting the exact thing that brought you here. We all have our own different principles and values which can be very distinct from one another. Don't emulate someone else's. I will never advise you to do that. Form your own values and principles. Look for something that would be important to you, something you can easily uphold. That is the only way you would be able to become emotionally intelligent overnight.

Lastly, always believe in yourself and your abilities. If you don't believe in yourself, no one will. At the end of the day, you are all you have left, thus, better start seeing the potentials in you. Better start seeing the possibilities surrounding you and making good use of them to your own benefit. If you believe you can do it, then nothing should stand in your way of success. All you need to have is a whole lot of determination, commitment, and patience. The rest will be history in no time.

Believe in your abilities and the whole world would see

you for what you truly are, and that is someone who is emotionally intelligent. This is the secret recipe no master of Emotional Intelligence would tell you. Many of them would start quoting authors and popular scholars just to make their simple point sound cumbersome. But, if you truly listen attentively to what they have been spewing, then you would realize that believing in oneself is a very important part of mastering your emotions.

Boosting your Emotional Intelligence overnight is very possible. The journey of a thousand miles begins with a bold step, and that bold step is what you need as regards boosting your Emotional Intelligence. If you are ready, determined, and committed, nothing will stop you from achieving your goals. Be that as it may, the next chapter will delve into Emotional Intelligence and relationships. I know this is the chapter you've all been waiting for, so just flip on over.

Chapter Six

7 Tips to Increase Your EQ for Better Relationships

The primary aim of Emotional Intelligence is to be able to maintain and manage better relationships with the people around you. Either at work or at home, in whatsoever situation you find yourself in, the ability to maintain and manage these connections lies with us. Additionally, the way we hold on to a relationship also determines how well we cherish that relationship. For example, the way we would hold the connection between us and our best friends dear is definitely different from the way we hold the connection between us and our co-workers.

A relationship is all that matters in today's world. No matter how you turn it, you will realize that we alone can't live in the state of autarky no matter how hard we try. We can't stay isolated forever. There is always a need for us to interact with one another. Now, this is where Emotional Intelligence comes in. It helps us foster our relationship with friends and family with an understanding of our emotions. It believes that if you can truly keep your emotions in check, then there is no limit to the things you would achieve and conquer in the world today.

As a matter of fact, Emotional Intelligence is not just referring to or preaching the management and control of one's emotion alone, it cut across the management and influence of the emotions of others too. If we can achieve this feat, then managing relationships and connections shouldn't be hard to pull off. In an organizational atmosphere where 60% of the workers are male and 40% of the workers are female, a test was carried out on the level of the workers' Emotional Intelligence and the result was highly predictable.

Almost every male in the organization got above 70% of the score, with the females failing woefully to a very large extent (please note that this is not in any way a direct or indirect jibe to the feminist). According to the Emotional Intelligence experts, they believed the result of the test was highly correct due to the fact that women often fail to separate their emotions from anything they do, including their professional career.

A career woman today with everything going on for her would still feel emotional towards something. It's the natural order of things with women. They are naturally bound to think toward emotion. But with Emotional Intelligence, things can be different this time. They can have a balance between themselves as regards being emotional, thereby, making them become masters of their emotions.

When we react to certain issues in our relationships, we

tend to go overboard with things. For example, in order to get the much-needed attention that we seek, we try to build mountains out of nothing. In the end, we might get the attention we had craved, but at a very costly price. Our relationship can end up getting strained or even severed at most. And if at all we are still lucky to have the relationship, then our connection would definitely get weak.

When you see two people growing all over each other, then you should assume they just got lucky to have found each other. As a matter of fact, both of them must have passed through challenging phases in the course of their relationship but still maintained patience and perseverance. There are occasions where only one person in the relationship is the mature one. There are cases where the man or the woman might be an emotionally intelligent fellow. Now, that is what it takes for a relationship to be as strong as ever. If you want your relationships with people to stand the test of time, then you really need to understand how they operate.

You need to know when their off moments are, you need to know what drives them crazy, and you need to know what they feel at all times. That is the only way you would be abreast with the happenings in their life and the best way to do this is to learn to read their emotions correctly. We would then be able to help them out when the need arises. We would be able to tend to them whenever they feel down. We would be able to know what they want at the right time. We would also be able to predict their next move even without them telling us. If we are a very good master of emotions, we would make new relationship more easily than we lose them.

I once dated a very immature lady and I must confess that the relationship was really hectic. As a master of Emotional Intelligence, I made sure I overlooked her shortcomings and mistakes because of the likeness I had had for her. Thus, I became the mature one in the relationship. Along the line, she started complaining that I was too expressionless. According to her, she didn't even know my emotions anymore. Sometimes, she would want to irritate me by force, but being a master of my own emotions, I had always managed to stay clear of trouble.

I was able to manipulate and sway our relationship through the hurdles of life. But it got to a point where I just got tired of being the mature one. Emotional Intelligence might guide me via that journey but my will, patience, and commitment kept my sanity. You need to have a mixture of all these key ingredients in order to have a successful relationship with another person. Emotional Intelligence may help you open up pathways for a successful relationship, but if the other person is also not willing to adjust or control their own emotions, then your effort might just seem fruitless.

Many great relationships today are built on the ability to checkmate our emotions. When both of us are masters of our own emotions, there is no rock our relationship won't surpass. No matter how stiff the obstacles may be, we will always sail pass it. Now, what will this chapter do? This particular chapter will help you see possible ways in which you can improve your relationship. It will help you see how you can save your relationship from dying off. And it will also show you ways to which you can reconnect with your friends and family in cases of lost connection.

1. **Avoid Negative Thoughts and Emotions:** The only possible way you can see potential and goodness in your relationships with other people is by always focusing on the brighter side. When you always immerse yourself in the possibilities surrounding your relationships, then your relationships will thrive. Now, how do you go about this? It's simple. Just try and erase any negative thoughts in your mind towards your relationships. When you do that, there will be little or no problems at all. And if these problems arise, you will be filled with more than enough zeal to tackle them.

Pushing back negative thoughts and emotions about our relationships can be quite difficult. For example, losing the trust you share with a person can end up spoiling the relationship. We all know that trust is the foundation of every relationship. Without this trust, there can really be no connection between us and others. You can imagine building a relationship with someone you don't trust. That will just end up being disastrous.

A good relationship thrives on good emotions and thoughts. If at all times, all you guys think are good thoughts about one another, there would certainly be no issue at all. Although this is easier said than done, you can at least give it a shot. I know these negative emotions and thoughts will surely cross your path, but the way and manner in which you handle yourself during these events will determine how far the relationship will go.

Janice and Wayne were good friends in the university. Their meeting was as a result of a strange circumstance which led to their unbreakable bond and connection over the past two years. One can boldly say that they are each other's best friend. However, Janice saw Wayne smoking weed and she as a person has an irritation for the plant, let alone the users of it. Instead of telling Wayne how she felt immediately as Emotional Intelligence would have strongly supported, she kept it to herself.

Now, their connection began getting weaker by the day because of the negative thoughts and emotions Janice had gathered and accumulated in her mind about Wayne. It is important to note that being honest with others is an important attribute of Emotional Intelligence. Yet, Janice wasn't. She kept her thoughts and opinions to herself, thereby, feeding herself with nothing but negative emotions and thoughts. These same emotions would be the tool for breaking the bond between them.

If Janice had been honest with Wayne, if Janice had called Wayne to the table and emptied her guts, and if Janice had voiced out, their relationship of two years wouldn't have hit the rocks. You never can tell if that was Wayne's first time smoking pot. You never can tell if he was being cajoled, bullied or brainwashed by the other kids into smoking with them. But instead, Janice jumped to a conclusion - a conclusion that ended their relationship for good.

Be that as it may, we should always learn to look at the situation very closely before jumping to conclusions. We should always be sure we have our facts before allowing our thoughts and emotions to grow negatively. If at all our emotions end up taking the better side of us, then we should not forget to be honest with our partners. At least they deserve that from us. Always see the brighter side of things no matter how shrewd they might look. That is the only way we can be sure that we aren't making a mistake.

2. **Listen More, Choose Your Words Carefully, and be a Good Communicator:** Have you ever seen a working

relationship where dialogue wasn't practiced more than usual? Many people forget that this tool works wonders in a relationship, especially in times of crisis and turmoil. When everything seems to be going south in your relationships, the best way to get things back on track is to be a good communicator. And what does a good communicator do? He listens attentively and speaks perfectly when the need arises.

Believe it or not, dialogue is the best way to foster your relationships. With the mixture of both dialogue and Emotional Intelligence, there would be nothing stopping you from establishing any form of connection in your relationships. Even in your place of work, you should always endeavor to be a good communicator amidst your fellow employees or employers. That way, you will be given the much-needed respect you deserve and the working relationships will improve rapidly.

As an emotionally intelligent person, what you should always be working toward is to become a better version of who you were yesterday. When you meet new people, your words should clarify how different you are from the rest. When you talk, you should be mindful of the emotions of others. Don't say things that will hurt them in any way, no matter crazy your emotions might be. The focus of Emotional Intelligence is to keep your emotions in check anyway. Be sure to do a good job.

What if you had a bad day? How would you manage your emotions afterward? Emotionally intelligent people always proffer solution to their emotional problems and to that of the people around them. If ever you find yourself being stuck at a particular point, then don't feel bad at all. Instead, look for a way around the solution. Additionally, when you are relating to others around you, you should learn to be a good listener. The floor isn't meant for you alone. Let others have a say, too. That is the only way your relationships will flourish.

3. **Be Empathetic at all Times:** What more do you need to know about Emotional Intelligence if not being empathetic toward everyone around you? The ability to know what others are feeling is a rare gift mastered by only emotionally intelligent people in the world. If you possess this gift, then kudos to you. Look for clues and pointers in you aren't very close to the person but still, care about him or her. Stay calm and collected each time you are around that person. That is the only way you will be able to know what their true emotions are.

Some people are very good at masking their emotions from others. No matter how hard you try to take a peep into their inner self, they just won't budge. Nonetheless, you still need to be emotionally attentive to such people. You need to show them genuine love and care. That is the only language they understand. This is because these set of people find it very hard to trust people. Thus, you need to earn trust. Soothe them with your words of encouragement and support. Show them what life will be like if only they can trust and open up their inner feelings.

Empathy in the professional sense has also been a driving force in today's world. It is believed that many top companies in the country today now focus on the Emotional Intelligence levels of their employees. They believe if one is filled with empathy, then there would certainly be a good working relationship between the employee and their clients. In other words, it would mean additional revenue for these companies. If these employees can continue to keep their clients happy, then it's a good thing for the company.

Sometimes, before we truly understand the emotions running through some people, we need to actually place ourselves in their position. We would need to first sit back and watch how everything played out from their angle. If we keep looking at things from our own angle, then we are bound to always misunderstand the emotions of others, and that negates the principle of empathy.

4. **Know Your Push Buttons:** I would strongly advise you to keep your push buttons far from where others might see them. In fact, bury them deep if you can. That is the

only way you won't get stressed or even tensed over little things. You really need to make sure you are familiar with your breaking points. Always make sure you are in control of them. And if you can't control them, then at least be sure to always be conscious of them. That way, you will be able to apply the much needed precautionary measures when the need arises.

If weed turns you off completely, they always make sure you ring it out to the ears of everyone around you. That way, they will be able to avoid using it around you. If drinking is what irritates you, then make sure your circle is clean and sober. You need to set boundaries for yourself in order to have prosperous and fruitful relationships with the people around you. And if you feel you can make compromises, feel free to do so.

Thus, let us know our weak points for a better relationship. If you are dating someone who knows all your push buttons, then that person would know exactly what to avoid so as not to get you filled with negative emotions. Well, except in cases where that person might start pushing those buttons intentionally. But as an emotionally intelligent person, you should be able to tell the difference. Whichever way it is, always make sure you have a precautionary measure to your push buttons.

5. **Approach Adversities Maturely:** One important thing

that accompanies all relationships is ups and downs. There will definitely be good times and bad times. But remember, when the good times come, don't get too carried away. Instead, prepare for the bad. I'm not saying you shouldn't enjoy the good time while it lasts. As a matter of fact, I would advise you to enjoy every bit of it - but not without preparing yourself for the bad that may follow.

When the time comes for the bad moments, your preparation will now come in handy. You will now be able to bounce back from the tribulations like it's nothing. When I mean preparation, I'm referring to mental and emotional preparation. Now that is where Emotional Intelligence comes in. Emotional Intelligence will equip you emotionally and mentally to withstand any obstacles and adversities you might face.

Instead of reacting weakly, wrongly, and emotionally, we will be able to react maturely and properly. Instead of gathering negative emotions and thoughts in our hearts, we will be able to focus on the possibilities around us. We will be able to think positive. Thus, always keep the optimism, even when things aren't looking good in your relationship. The way you approach your problems is definitely the way you would address them.

6. **Reflect:** Always reflect on the events and situations that

have happened in your relationships over the past years. Reflections are signs of overcoming our troubles and obstacles. Reflection comes after overcoming the trials that may have made our relationships unbearable. It is important to know that reflections do not make us weak, nor do they make us vulnerable, instead they make us even more mature and wise.

Only great men reflect back to their previous actions. That way, they will be able to pick up corrections in case of future reoccurrence. Along the line of reflecting on our relationships, we would realize the strengths and weaknesses of our actions. We would be able to replay our actions again and again until we learn from them. If you are dating a temperamental person who loses his or her cool at the slightest provocation, the best way for you to approach such a person is to stay calm and understand their emotions.

Afterward, you can take your time to reflect on the events that left you puzzled. Make sure you weigh your strengths and weaknesses during your moment of reflection. Think deep about what started the misunderstanding in the first place. Do not cultivate the habit of playing the blame game. Instead, know where your faults lie and work on them. Reflections are created for just one reason, and that is to be a better version of what you are now. Reflect well and make good use of them.

7. **Admit and Accept Your Fault when you are Wrong:** It is important to know that accepting one's faults doesn't make you smaller or inferior. Instead, it will make you a person with a big heart. When we know our faults, the best thing to do is to admit to them and make amends immediately before it gets out of hand. Thanks to Emotional Intelligence, accepting our faults and knowing where our mistakes lie brings us closer to our friends and family. We will even become closer, with ours bond getting stronger by the day.

Many believe that relationships are meant to be made and broken. Well, that is just not true. Relationships are indeed meant to be kept and improved upon. Are you having issues maintaining your relationships on a professional or personal level? Then have you tried Emotional Intelligence? If no, then this chapter is written just for you. Give Emotional Intelligence a shot in your relationships this time, and you will be shocked at how amazing things would flow.

Chapter Seven

19 Ways to Improve Your Emotions in 2019

2019 is a year filled with new, exciting adventures, as well as challenges. It is a year which further exposes the 21st century as the age of technological revolutions, medical breakthroughs, scientific innovations, and so much more. Now, let's take a very long jump from all these great and abstract feats. How about relationships? How has 2019 become the new age for a modernized and sophisticated form of relationships? How has 2019 fashioned the connection of one person to another? Has it really made a reasonable impact in this direction?

Without mincing many words, it won't be far from the truth if we say 2019 has also contributed its own quota to the developing of relationships and connections within the world. People now see relationships, connections, and Spirituality in a whole new light. Instead of the traditional methods of growing and maintaining relationships, there have been a whole lot of improved tips and techniques which have proven to be far more effective and efficient. Now, this is where Emotional Intelligence comes into play.

As a brand new idea that was conceived over a decade by

a popular scholar, Emotional Intelligence has thrived over the years with lots of people adopting this idea and building upon the foundation. As an advocate of emotional control, Emotional Intelligence goes deeper than you can imagine. It touches other aspects like Spirituality, connections, relationships, motivation, success, and so much more. According to the tenets, if we can truly control our emotions, if we can truly keep our feelings in check, and if truly we can understand our feelings as well as the feelings of others, then there is no limit to what we will achieve.

Be that as it may, 2019 comes with its own distractions and complications, too. It is as if the more it becomes glamorous, the more it becomes even more distracting. The world today is filled with lots of these side attractions that may sway you off the path to becoming a master of your own emotions. For example, there are now a whole lot of trigger points which would make you lose focus or concentration even without knowing it. Thanks to globalization, the world today has now contracted into one whole bunch.

New inventions, ideas, and innovations might not really go down well with you, thereby making you lose yourself in the process. I can still recall vividly when the current United States of America's president, in the person of Donald Trump, won the election by defeating Hilary Clinton to emerge victoriously. My opposite neighbor, who had always carried himself well, lost his calm that same moment right in my presence. I must say, I'd never seen a man get so stressed, tensed, angry, and frustrated all at the same time.

He swore and cursed for almost an hour before he could get a grip of himself. I totally understood his frustration, probably because he is Mexican and was highly concerned about Donald Trump's policies that negate the growth of his race in the United States. Now, this reaction from someone who had always comported himself well got me thinking. Was 2019 really that different? Or had we all evolved to a point where Emotional Intelligence hardly works?

It didn't take me long to figure the whole thing out. 2019 comes with its own complications indeed, and the frustrations we get from these complications are mostly stored up inside of us, causing stress and anxiety. When the slightest thing around us starts irritating us, then we really need to go back into our spiritual realm. That way, we will be able to reconnect with ourselves, thereby, going to our principles and values which have marked our true self from the beginning. If we are losing touch with our Emotional Intelligence, then we need to prepare our minds and focus on the possibilities around us.

We need to regain the consciousness that once held our emotions. We need to really understand the basis that defines our emotional breakdown or meltdown. That way, we would be able to know what our emotions are and what they really entail. Sometimes, we get so worked up due to the pressures we might have faced at work. Some of us work three to four shift, just to make hands meet, thus, there would be very little or no tolerance at all on our part. Additionally, a simple coffee expresso machine or toaster might go bad without our knowledge, thus, dashing our hope for an early morning coffee.

This disappointment might not go down well with us, thus, making us lose our cool. Little things like that seldom have a way of making us lose our self in the process. When this happens, keeping calm is the best way to go about it. This is what every master of Emotional Intelligence will tell you to do. Remember, we can't control how we feel, but we can definitely control the outcome of those feelings. Now, it is your choice to either go berserk or act maturely. But trust me, the latter would be preferable.

It is understandable if you lose your cool over that espresso machine, especially if you are a low-income earner. There are lots of thoughts that would definitely go through your head. You would start imagining how to go about fixing it or getting a new one if it's old and worn out. Nonetheless, using your Emotional Intelligence to tackle the situation would be a lot better.

Now, what will this chapter do? This chapter will

familiarize you with the face of Emotional Intelligence and how to improve on it in the year 2019. There are lots of ways in which Emotional Intelligence can be improved this year, especially judging from the present face of things. Losing your cool and giving in to your emotions is quite easy with the present state of the world today, so how do we really improve our Emotional Intelligence in 2019?

1. **Keep Everything Normal:** When we tend to keep our tempos up, there is every tendency that we might lose our emotions. Always try to stay calm whenever you feel uncomfortable. That way, your temperature would go down. Additionally, you can also give in to more sleep. When we retire early, we tend to get ourselves refreshed. Our mental and physical health would improve beyond recognition.

   Additionally, we would also recommend you to keep your room at a normal temperature. Make sure everything is set for you to have a sound sleep. Sometimes, we tend to get stressed with the harsh weather conditions. We are likely to get more tensed in a very hot atmosphere. Thus, keep the atmosphere normal as it would help you become a better version of what you were yesterday.

2. **Be Bold to Try out New Things:** Be bold enough to test new waters. Don't just confine yourself to a particular spot or position. Challenge yourself to try out new

boundaries. Thank God 2019 brings out new things around us; make sure you use them well. Be sure to look for new adventures. Be sure to test yourself beyond your areas of specialization. If your emotions are just a little beyond control, then I would recommend you know what drives it crazy and what keeps it in control.

That is the only way you would improve. Know your boundaries first, and then start working toward progressing with them. Start working towards moving past the boundaries of your emotions. In other words, try out new things. Try out new hobbies. Go out and make new friends. Make sure you meet new people. Engage yourself in your new activities. If this happens, there are certain ways in which trying out new things would serve as a stress reliever.

When you try out new things, you will be immersed with the mysteries surrounding them. These mysteries that surround them will be the mechanism that will push you into becoming more confident with your emotions.

3. **Create New Circles:** 2019 is a year of plush and plenty. It is a year filled with life and prosperity. Thus, why not be among those that would explore this exciting and amazing year? Make new friends, meet new people, and create new circles or group. For example, if you are a regular member of a certain mental health social group, how about trying out new exciting groups, too? How

about exploring what the other groups have to offer?

Now, always put it at the back of your mind that people will always want to interact with you even if you push them away. In this modern world, some people just don't take no for an answer. You might be shocked to discover that it is these same people that are most amazing to connect with. Connecting with them would give you no problem at all. Notwithstanding, improve your Emotional Intelligence by increasing your social circle.

In case you don't know, having a lot of friends and family to connect with would kill off any spirit of loneliness in you. Interacting and sharing ideas with your friends and family would help make you feel great in the end. When you have someone to talk to, someone to relate with, and someone to connect with, you will come to find life very easy - trust me.

4. **Paint or Color if You Feel Stressed:** This is one method that works all the time. A lot of people believe doing what you love at your moment of stress will help drop the stress tempos and levels. This is very true. Additionally, what you love doing in the time of stress and loneliness is quite different from what others love doing. Coincidentally, if taking a walk or listening to music is your thing, then there is a chance that this same walk or music can be a thing for several people too.

But one thing that works well is painting and coloring. First, it helps you get back to normal. It brings your levels down whenever they are too high, thereby, making you feel amazing in the end. Additionally, painting your fears and worries away can also be in the form of a new type of art. You get to make yourself feel alright and you also get to add the painting to your collection. Now, that is a win-win situation.

Whenever you feel tense, stressed, and want to build on your Emotional Intelligence, painting and coloring is one way out of it. Your stress levels would determine the colors you pick. And one way or the other, your mind would just seem to contract back to normal. If ever you feel uncomfortable or angry over a certain decision or mistake you've made, then I strongly recommend you go into painting. Pour your frustration into it and you will come out as good as new.

5. **Become Incommunicado if the Need Arises:** There are times in life when we just want to be alone, no matter how hard we try to stay focused and relate with the people around us. We just seldom feel disconnected with these loads of people around us, who are probably trying hard to make us feel better or even get our attention. Seriously, it's not all about the connection we feel for one another. Sometimes, the best way to become the best

version of ourselves is by staying disconnected from all things.

That is the only way we will be able to move forward. That is the only way we would be able to realize what the problem really is. Sometimes, all we need is time alone to refresh ourselves. Feel free to stay off the radar for a while. It's part of the process of becoming a better version of yourself. Now, in this computerized and technologically advanced world, how can one stay off the grid? It's pretty simple.

Start by going to a secluded area and stay in solitude. Stay clear off your phones and gadgets. In fact, stay clear off any form of notification devices that may enable others to reach you. The amount of time you stay in solitude is mostly determined by how much time you need to get yourself back to normal. And remember, all you need is just a little bit of peace and quiet. The rest will work itself out naturally.

6. **Eat Good Food and Diet if You Can:** There is a certain food that would enable you to react in a certain way or even improve and decrease our level of Emotional Intelligence as time progresses. When you eat something you shouldn't have, there is every tendency that the food you have taken in will do some damage in you. For example, taking in much sugar would cause quite a lot of damage to your system, even though you still need sugar.

Also, there are some foods we would strongly recommend for you if at all you are trying to work on your Emotional Intelligence. How about adding Omega-3 Fatty Acids in your daily diet? Trust me; they are very good for your Emotional Intelligence levels. They will help maintain your levels as well as increase your interactive rate with the people around you.

So, what kind of food should we consume? Obviously, food that contains this particular acid would be more advisable. For example, salmon, flaxseed, walnuts, and other oil supplements are just perfect for you. In as much as they help the body in making sure the depression rate is at the minimal, they also help in giving the body a whole lot of other nutrients that will come in handy. Eat what you must, but always think Omega-3 Fatty Acids first.

7. **Exercise and Aerobics Would Help, Too:** I haven't seen a book or heard someone that had made an important criticism or complaint against exercising the body. With a whole lot of books stressing the benefits that come with exercising the body, even a dumb person knows how effective and efficient exercise can be in our lives. Wither you are taking a mere walk or doing a rigorous workout in the nearby gym, it's all to the realization of one thing – a perfect body.

Now, how does exercise relate to improved Emotional

Intelligence? I'll tell you. When you exercise the body, your body attracts healthiness in return. In other words, our body ensures that every possible system in it functions properly. Additionally, exercising the body helps keep the body circulation rate normal and when the circulation rate becomes normal, our mood becomes better. Aside from that, you would also be taking good care of yourself.

Exercise works wonders in our body in more ways than you can imagine. It stretches out the muscles and joints, it relaxes the body, and it ensures the body is in a good working condition. When you exercise your body, it will make you look fit. In other words, give you a dream body, thus giving you the confidence to be who you want to be around your friends and family. That way, you will definitely be motivated, inspired, and feel amazing.

8. **Clear Your Head with Walks and Strolls:** Always cultivate the habit of going out for a walk or stroll. You can either do this alone or with friends and family if you want to. Instead of staying bottled up inside your apartment in solitude, you can also go out there and embrace the world. Taking a walk around the park, strolling the neighborhood, or even jogging to the fields would help you clear your head. It would help you reduce tension and stress.

Are you angry about a particular event or situation?

Then walk it over. Are you mad about something you did and weren't really proud of? Then stroll over it. Walking around or just taking a stroll would help relieve the stress you are feeling. It would kill off any feelings of loneliness. And trust me; there is a good chance of you meeting someone new. There is a big possibility of you connecting with someone.

Meanwhile, ensure these walks and strolls are in your schedule, so as not to inconvenience yourself in the end. Go out there and enjoy nature. Take a walk to the park or woods and see nature firsthand. You would be surprised at how amazing you would feel before heading back home. Be that as it may, walking solves your problem of fatigue, reduces depression to the minimum, and boosts your level of Emotional Intelligence.

9. **Never Let That Smile Leave Your Face:** Your smile is your selling point. It is your most enticing weapon, which you can use anytime you feel uncomfortable, stressed, or even lost. When things start getting out of control, then you should start thinking of flashing that set of teeth out for people to see. Smiling is a gesture that keeps us out of trouble. Even in the most tensed situation of our lives, a single smile would make everything become normal.

Now, wouldn't you rather smile than go through a whole

lot of hurt? Wouldn't you rather smile to avoid those erupting emotions in you from damaging the good relationships you had toiled to keep? Even when we don't feel too good about a certain decision concerning us, we shouldn't show our outburst in an inconveniencing way. If we know we can't contain the emotions or turn the situation to our own benefit, then we should just smile over it.

A smile would reassure the other partner in a relationship that all is well. A smile would rekindle the connection that might have seemed to be lost. With just a smile, you can melt even the hardest of hearts. We can get through to even those that aren't ready to open up if only we just smile at every possible situation. That would only make our mood even better. A beautiful smile will make sure our mind stays calm and our heart rate normal.

10. **Learn about Postures and Explore to the Best of Your Ability:** Emotional Intelligence comes with staying confident and being confident comes with carrying yourself well in an amazing way. This is where having a good posture comes into play. Make 2019 your year of good living. Make 2019 your year of great confidence and power. It is important to know that when we tend to act smart around the people we care about, our relationships will definitely thrive.

But when we start acting sluggishly, when we start acting

dull and emotional, the relationship will suffer. Thus, sit properly at all times. Stand properly also. If you are walking, then walk properly, too. That is the only way you will be able to exude confidence which will lead to motivation, inspiration, and success. When you carry yourself with so much grace, people would want to really relate with you even more.

11. **Don't Joke with the Power of Vitamin D:** Allow Vitamin D be your best friend. Always make sure you get it in surplus so as to be able to hold your body and soul together. Immerse yourself in the power of the smiling sun. Afterward, watch yourself grow and remain ravishing. If we keep looking fresh and amazing, then there is no telling how much we will achieve in the year 2019.

When you take at least 15 minutes of your time to take in the brightness of the sun, your mood will definitely improve and your Emotional Intelligence will become just as sharp as that of any master. Remember, when the body is in good working conditions, nothing will be able to stop you from reaching the peak of your world.

12. **Plan a Retreat Sometime:** Your body needs every bit of relaxation you can give it. Sometimes, all we need to do is to go down a little in order to come out even stronger. Are you feeling tensed at work lately? Do you feel stuffed

at home with everything happening around you always getting the better side of you? Do you feel you are reaching a point in life where you just won't be able to take it anymore? Then plan a getaway.

You can plan a getaway with family, friends or even alone. This would definitely lift up your spirits and keep you motivated. You can also go on a spiritual journey. This would make you realize what truly lies ahead of you. Make sure you set this example in the year 2019. As a matter of fact, make it occasional. Find a place where you will always love to be and make sure you spend some time there, if not frequently, at least occasionally.

You would be surprised at how your emotions would drop to normal. A getaway would ease your mind as it will bring in relaxation. Trust me - depression would be very far away from your doorstep. Walk away temporarily from the troubles and crises in your life and things will definitely set out fine for you.

13. **Always be Grateful:** According to a wise saying, scaling gratitude will definitely lead to a higher altitude. A mind that is filled with gratitude would definitely receive nothing but joy and happiness in return. Thus, learn to cultivate this attitude within yourself. No matter how little anything might be, so long it affects your life positively, show gratitude. Be thankful always for what

you have, what you have become, and what you will be.

A mind that is filled with gratitude would know no greed, pain, and ego. It would be a mind filled with satisfaction, love, and joy. Now, that kind of mind is what you truly need in order to develop your Emotional Intelligence even further. In order to reassemble and reconnect with your inner self even better, you would need to have a mind devoid of ungratefulness, greed, and ingratitude.

Thus, I would recommend you take this seriously. Every day of your life, before you lay your back on the bed, make sure you reflect on the things that had happened to you all through that 24 hour timeline. Then think of the things you need to be thankful for. That way, your mind will be full of positivity, thereby, making your outlook also change for the better. A thankful soul is a blessed mind; never forget that.

14. **Keep Records of Things by Writing Your Experiences Down:** Whether you decide to keep a journal or a diary, just try and have something you can use to write your vital experiences down. There is always a great relief that comes with this journal keeping. Writing can be a way of keeping yourself abreast of the happenings in your life. It can also be a way of releasing the tensions and stress that have built up in you already.

A lot of masters of Emotional Intelligence would tell you this is a good way to bring your levels down. For example, if you have something bothering you at work or at home, then the best way to make yourself fell alright about it is to write it down somewhere. That way, you would be able to think of a way in which you can face them squarely. These tactics should be employed in 2019 if truly you want to improve your Emotional intelligence.

15. **Feel Free to say NO When the Need Arises:** This is the number one killer of every relationship out there. Because we might have a certain level of connection with our friends and family, we would now be obligated to make them feel special by any means necessary, even though it means inconveniencing ourselves in the end. This attitude of ours would definitely put us in trouble whether we like it or not.

We can't do everything all by ourselves. We can't go on making ourselves unhappy just because we want to please others. In the end, we will be losing ourselves without us even knowing. We should learn to stop cultivating this habit in the year 2019. Don't hesitate to say no whenever you feel unhappy, pressured, and tensed about a certain situation.

Stop making promises that would put you in trouble in the end. Let this year make a difference in your life. Before making a crucial decision that would make your life unbearable or might not benefit you in the long run, think deeply about it. And if you think you can't handle it, then kindly say NO. No one would hold a gun to your neck when this happens. Don't inconvenience yourself in order to please others. That will be emotionally unintelligent.

16. **Eat a Well-Balanced Diet at all Times:** Eating junk or fast foods can be quite disadvantageous to our bodies in the long run. Thus, we should always make sure we eat well in order to maintain a great body. When the body is in a good working condition, we will be able to react well to the happenings in our lives. I have seen people who get easily emotional due to an illness in their body.

Any time my father gets sick, we all know better than to act normal around him. During this phase, he gets easily paranoid and highly emotional at the same time. Thus, we always try to act extra carefully and extra cautious each time we are around him during this phase. As a bus driver, my dad had been accustomed to eating junk. Every morning, he would get a cheeseburger on his way to the bus park, skip the afternoon meal, and mostly eat all forms of pasta for dinner.

Always eat well no matter the schedule of your work and engagements. When you eat well, your body will respond well, there will be a smooth circulation running through you, and every other part will function perfectly well. Both your physical and mental health will be in great shape. Make sure your meals contain the six classes of food. That is one of the ways to stay in great shape.

17. **Start with Smaller Goals before Advancing to Bigger Ones:** Before the start of 2019, I'm sure you already had your New Year goals and objectives well mapped out. Now, take a good look at them. Do they include achieving bigger things? For example, do you plan on focusing more on the outside than the inside? Do you plan on making a lot of people smile out there? Does it include reconnecting with all lost connections?

If it does, then it's a good thing. But allow me to ask you some questions. Don't you feel those goals are too high for now? Don't you feel you need to really understand yourself and emotions first before understanding someone else's? Making people happy is cool, but have you made yourself happy? This is what I would want you to do, set your goals from this basis. Then build on them until you reach the peak of to your goals.

Start from scratch. You can only make an impact in the lives of others if you make an impact on yours. You can only understand people's emotions and be able to influence them for the better after you have mastered your own emotions. This is how Emotional Intelligence really works. Do this and you will be shocked at how much growth you will achieve all on your own.

Additionally, taking time to reflect on the things we had missed out last year wouldn't be a bad idea. After all, Emotional Intelligence is all about making the best out of your emotions by reflecting on them. In 2019, make sure you don't repeat the same mistakes. Make sure you program yourself into going for only goals that can be realistic and not the ones that are out of your reach. If we focus on what we can't achieve, it brings depression and failure into our lives. And if you feel the goals are important, feel free to break them into parts. That would make them easy to achieve.

18. **Know Your Mental State:** There is only one way in which we can stay abreast with our mental state and that is by getting ourselves educated about mental issues. If we are aware of our mental issues, we will surely know the stages at which our emotions can be or are currently in. When we know about our mental issues, we will be able to adopt a new way, if possible coin our own methods in bringing down our mental levels back to normal when the need arises.

Having an idea of mental issues will put us ahead of our own emotions. We will be able to tell when and how we feel at a particular time. That way, we would be able to navigate our way through depression, emotional trauma, stress, and so much more. However, if you feel what you are going through is far more than what the little knowledge you know can handle, then feel free to try even more sophisticated means.

19. **Always Engage Yourself in Something You Love Doing:** Never stop doing what you love, especially if it leaves a smile on your face each time. Whenever you feel down, you should be able to calm yourself with that thing that you love doing. If it is shopping that makes you lively, then go for it so long you have the means to. If it is music that brings the better part of you out into the world, then go into it fully. Don't allow anything stop you from doing what you love doing this year.

When we probably excel at something, then it means we are good at it. Now, that thing, be it yoga, swimming, dancing, and so on, can become a part of us. For example, whenever you feel tensed and you know whistling is the only way to make you feel better, then feel free to whistle. However, you wouldn't want to start whistling loud in your place of work. Just don't stop doing what brings life into you. Continue making yourself happy. That way, your Emotional Intelligence will definitely improve.

So far, 2019 has been a noisy and busy year with lots of events, situations, and activities going on around the globe. If the same thing applies to your own personal life, then I would suggest you find ways to improve yourself and your Emotional Intelligence this year in order to be able to contain yourself and the people around you. Pay close attention to this chapter and make sure you immerse yourself to the 19 special tips we outlined on improving your Emotional Intelligence.

Chapter Eight

The Little-Known Time-Tested Principles to Follow If You Want to Persuade Others

The power of persuasion is an outstanding trait you would only find in 1 out of 20. When one possesses this power, then one is said to have mastered emotions completely. Aside from self-awareness, which deals with identifying your emotions and knowing that they exist, self-control comes next which also deals with understanding your emotions in order to keep your relationships intact. When you have the ability to control the outcome of your own emotions, then everything will definitely fall in line for you.

Empathy comes next. Ripple by ripple, we would now start developing particular care and feeling toward the people around us. What is the use of understanding our own emotions without understanding the emotions of others? When we understand them, our relationships will definitely progress. We will know how they feel at any particular moment even before they start telling us what the problem is. We would be able to approach anybody that comes our way the right way no matter how shrewd the situation may be.

We would be able to know when to shoot our shots and when to stay in our shell.

Finally, social skills are the last phase to it and that deals with the power of persuasion. In other words, you have an influence in the life of people around us. Emotional Intelligence would definitely help show you how to exert an influence in the life of others when the need arises. Darlington is a top chef at a prestigious restaurant in town. Though he was the assistant chief chef, people really preferred him to any other person in the restaurant. When Darlington takes orders, he has the ability to influence the customer's decisions for the better.

Darlington would make sure he gets you the best of what you want. It's like he knows his customers' taste buds even before they enter. Thus, when he left the restaurant to open his own makeshift food truck, 80% of the customers left with him. As a matter of fact, Darlington is now an underdog with lots of investors ready to take a chance on him. Now, that is the power of persuasion via Emotional Intelligence, when we have the ability to help people see the possibilities around them. When we have the ability to help others realize what they have been missing which is just right in front of them the whole time, then we can boldly hit our chest to have possessed the power of persuasion.

The power of persuasion comes with being influential.

When you are always geared toward making the life of the people around you improve for the better, you are definitely making an impact that would leave you to be more influential than before. It takes just a little bit of sweet talk and a very large amount of Emotional Intelligence for one to be able to influence others. The power of persuasion lies with great men and women, men and women of valor and honor, men and women that have the ability to understand the emotions of the people around them and turn them to their own advantage.

In your relationships, if you hold this power, then I would suggest you wield it appropriately. Some people can be very cunning and greedy. They can also misuse this power in order to achieve their own selfish desires. For example, one man that has greatly misused this power in the course of history is Adolf Hitler himself. This man was popularly known to have possessed true power of persuasion when he rose from nothing to the top of the ranks in Germany. Thanks to his persuasion skills, he was able to influence the whole country into doing his bidding.

Now, what will this chapter do? This chapter will help sensitize you with the different persuasion principles out there. It will help you see persuasion for what it really is and how to further improve on it by following the well-tested principles, philosophical theories, and so much more. Be that as it may, when we look at the people around us closely, we will be able to predict who they are and what they want. We will be able to predict what they are really made of. It is important to know that everyone is configured separately, thus for us to really understand how their emotions would be toward certain situations, we would really need to first understand how they are wired.

I believe this is where we ask those questions that have been disturbing our minds over the years, yeah? We now begin to ask how some people we know can become so persuasive. How can some people be so good at it? Is being emotionally intelligent their topmost secret? How do we go about it? Would I be able to master the power of persuasion within the shortest possible time?

There are lots of techniques and principles one can use in mastering the power of persuasion. These techniques and principles have also being used one way or the other by today's world leaders, be it religious, political, social, business, and so much more. The power of persuasion is a rare gift that will take you places if harnessed properly. It will help you build your relationship from scratch if applied appropriately. And it will help you attain the heights you have always craved for.

I will categorically share these principles into different segments so as to allow you to become familiar with the skills and tactics. First, I would explain the Basics, then move on to General Rule, and finally the Personal Inborn Skills.

The Basics

1. **Wrong Assumptions:** This is one problem and misconception that has tarnished the image of the power of persuasion. A lot of people believed this act has to do with brainwashing and manipulation. This assumption is very wrong. When you influence the decisions of others positively, then you are simply being persuasive. You are making the person see things in another dimension without sugarcoating your words with lies and falsehood.

   Unlike manipulation and brainwashing, where you would have to be cunning and deceitful, being persuasive is a very clean source of being influential. Where manipulation and brainwashing come with the use of force, with making one do what he or she doesn't want to do, and with hurting someone into doing your bidding, persuasion simply deals with the art of making people see pass their short-sightedness. You would make them see the light.

2. **No One is Unpersuadable:** No matter how shrewd you might think you are, there is still a part of you that can be persuaded, whether you like it or not. All that is needed is to reach that inner part of you that is still soft. Thus, no one is free from the claws of persuasion. It all depends on

the way the person approaches you, the timing in which the person might approach you and the situation at hand.

The power of persuasion works on a long term process. First, you need to gain the trust of the people you would want to influence and this might take a very long time. For example, during elections, politicians would want to build a lasting relationship with the electorates as they decide the winners of every election. If you get your act right and punch the necessary buttons, you will definitely influence even the hardest of hearts.

3. Know the Right Timing: You can't just go all Barrack Obama on people at their most emotional moments. You might end up receiving a punch on the face if you try that. The timing is really important whenever you want to influence the decisions of the people around you. This is, in fact, the best way to make persuasion work. Focus on the timing, know when to strike, and the rest will be history. It's all about the timing with persuasion. When we are sure of the timing, you will be able to move even the hardest of hearts.

General Rule

4. **Leveraging Reciprocation:** There is a popular saying that goes like this; one good turn deserves another. When you are extremely and selflessly good toward another person,

then that person will feel obliged to return the favor in time, no matter how long it may take. The one good you have done will be outlined and stored in the heart of that person. This is just how we are being configured.

Now, how about making good use of this advantage? How about turning this long chain of gratitude to your own benefit? You can help someone out today and use that opportunity of reciprocation to collect a bigger return afterward. They would gladly give you a helping hand knowing fully well that they would also get help back from you in the future when the need arises. The chain goes on and on.

5. **Persistence is the Key:** When you know what you want, then the best way to go about it is to keep being persistent about it until you make a breakthrough. When you constantly stay glued to your persuasion skills, others are more likely to give in and start seeing things from your point of view. One of the key attributes that must be possessed by someone who possesses the power of persuasion is continuous persistence.

This is the key ingredient of every leader out there in the world. They would stay glued to their beliefs and opinions until their message is passed to every corner of their region. Be like these leaders in order to be persuasive. Abraham Lincoln still remained resolute to his beliefs even after losing lots of elections and the people he held dear. Even to the point of his assassination, he never swayed away from his beliefs. Now, that is real persuasion.

6. **Set Your Goals and Expectations:** The power of persuasion also deals with making other people believe and trust you no matter how the situation can be. If you can persuade them, then you are obviously asking them to take a chance in your well-set goals and expectations. At the end of the day, if you deliver, then the persuasion power comes in handy. But in cases where you fail to meet these expectations, then you can just start persuading all over again.

7. **The Assumption in Persuasion is Wrong:** Assumption is a key enemy to persuasion. When we start assuming things, then we fail to see the purpose of persuasion as a whole. Instead of assuming, why not allow ourselves just do the needful? Instead of assuming for others, why not let nature take its course?

Personal Skills

8. **Flexibility:** He or she that is most flexible possesses the power of persuasion. As a matter of fact, children also possess great powers of persuasion with their childish attitudes. For example, when a child wants something badly and wasn't given it, he or she will resort to all

forms of tricks in order to get that thing. The child might start crying even without anyone beating him or her. The child might even start pleading or becoming charming just to get it.

Now that is how great men think and react with persuasion. Persuasion is an art - an important one that deals with being flexible. You have to think of more than one way to influence another person. Thus, the more flexible your behavior can be, the better you will be at being persuasive.

9. **Be a Good Communicator:** Have you ever seen a leader who isn't good with words? Have you ever seen a leader without the command of good communication skills? All leaders possess the power of communication. That is the only way they can reach their followers. Now, when you apply this principle in your own life, lines will definitely fall in place for you. If you cannot reach even the dumbest of people, then you are not cut out for this kind of skill.

10. **Be Calm and Collected Always:** This is an attribute that works perfectly with leaders. As a leader who possesses the power of persuasion, you need to be extremely calm at all times, especially in times of need. This is the trait which you can use to your own advantage. In times of adversity, always remember to stay calm. In times of troubles, always remember to stay calm. In times of

negativity, always stay positive. This will give hope to the people around you.

Every single concept has its own guiding principles. These principles are what would serve as the light that will illuminate the path towards that concept. Trust me - if you can follow these well-proven and well-tested principles to the letter, then you shouldn't worry about losing yourself on the way. The next chapter will focus on the controversies surrounding the negativity of Emotional Intelligence. You won't want to miss it.

Chapter Nine

The Dark Side of Emotional Intelligence

In as much as we have painted Emotional Intelligence white since the beginning of this book, it still doesn't mean that there is no supposed dark side to the subject matter. As a matter of fact, there is nothing in this life that doesn't come with the pros and cons of it. No matter how perfect it might turn out to be, there will always be a negative side to it, no matter how little it might be. This same point applies to Emotional Intelligence.

Over the past few chapters, we have focused our energy on explaining how much importance and benefit one can derive from Emotional Intelligence if only we had learned to master it. Without a doubt, our life would improve with it, our relationships would sail even higher, and our connection with our inner self would see no bounds. But at what expense would we achieve all these? At what expense would we benefit from all these?

When we focus on the benefits one would derive from Emotional Intelligence, we will easily be carried away without taking a second look at the bad side of it, that is, if this bad sides truly exist. If Emotional Intelligence solves our problem of an emotional outbreak, how about the effects it might leave? You won't find a lot of books, Internet materials, and studies that would focus on the negative part of Emotional Intelligence. It is as if they all had reached a consensus of neglecting this crucial part of Emotional Intelligence. If you would want to sell out an idea to the public, wouldn't it be more appropriate if you go out clean?

This chapter will focus its lens on the so-called negative aspects of Emotional Intelligence. It will sensitize you on the negative effects you might encounter on your journey toward being emotionally independent. Don't get it twisted; Emotional Intelligence is a very good thing. Acknowledging it, identifying it, understanding it, and using it to influence the decisions of the people around you is a very good trait we all would want to have. Some won't even mind killing for this power.

However, it comes with a price and this price is what I will delve into. According to a whole lot of people out there, Emotional Intelligence comes with its own blemish. Many have believed the subject matter to be misconstrued. They believe Emotional Intelligence doesn't really have the right basis to be studied either as intelligence or as a personal character. In the same vein, no matter how well we look at this argument, we would only agree that there is no clear demarcation.

While some people have been of the notion that Emotional Intelligence is actually an intelligence, due to the fact that it can be tested and measured, others just believe it is something that can only be gotten as a result of your in-built traits. Now, if the basis of Emotional Intelligence is not even known and established, how can anyone claim to even understand what Emotional Intelligence really entails? Although there had been numerous examples of world leaders that had been able to demonstrate the control of their emotions at it's best, would it be correct if we call that Emotional Intelligence?

The definition and constructiveness of Emotional Intelligence are not well taken according to some group of scholars. They believe Emotional Intelligence doesn't have a clear background as to the measurements and tests. There is a strange contradiction between these distinctions. How well should Emotional Intelligence be measured or tested? Is it as intelligence or as a behavior? It is one thing to exude this trait as intelligence and it is another to project the trait as a behavior. Thus, which one is correct? Quite controversial, isn't it?

Aside from this, many also believed that there are no guiding principles that explain the use of Emotional Intelligence. We had seen or heard of cases where a whole lot of people who had mastered their emotions and even possesses the power of persuasion had used this outstanding trait for the worst things ever. Instead of making good use of this amazing skill or trait into making the world a better place, they had abused it instead by using it to achieve their selfish aim.

Adolf Hitler is a very good example of this selfish use of Emotional Intelligence. Now the question is, how do we stop people from misusing this trait? Are there even any guiding values and principles surrounding the use of Emotional Intelligence? Believe it or not, in as much as many people believe that Emotional Intelligence does more good than harm, others are forced to believe otherwise. Thus, there is a controversial tussle between both thoughts as to which is actually correct.

If you judge these notions by their various points, you would agree with me that both of them are actually correct. Furthermore, there is no clear distinction as to what kind of behaviors or intelligence patterns are familiar with Emotional Intelligence. Although there have been ongoing studies that would shed more light on this aspect, one can still say there aren't enough yardsticks that can be used in showing one's emotional capabilities.

Emotional Intelligence is just about throwing unreasonable feat about controlling one's emotions or outcomes. The controversial belief that this utopian idea is possible should not be conceived by anyone. Many religious leaders would agree with this notion. They would tell you being emotional is a feeling that comes with our being. It is how we are being configured. If Eve wasn't emotional, we wouldn't be down here on earth. If Cain hadn't been emotional, we wouldn't have known sin.

This is from the religious point of view. Instead of us trying hard to perfect the mysteries of God, how about we just enjoy it and let it flow? It is only robots that can't possess emotions or feelings. Instead of depriving yourself of these feelings as they come, how about allowing them to manifest on their own? Additionally, many people believed that Emotional Intelligence gained momentum in recent years solely because of their social capabilities and not their scientific or emotional control.

The world today is going wide and wild, thus, there is a need for people to possesses the power to control and understand the emotions of others around them, not because of anything but because of living together in harmony. Now, with the recent development and technological advancement like the nuclear, atomic, and biological weapons that are possessed by various nations, there is a need for Emotional Intelligence. In order words, the world doesn't need Emotional Intelligence because of its so-called tenets and principles but because of order and harmony.

But how sure are we that this trait would be the rise of a new Hitler? In another controversial opinion, many believed that Emotional Intelligence is a cover-up for the exploitation and capitalization of the world by the world capitalist giants out there. In order to make the exploited feel better and to continue exploiting labor and the resources available for all, Emotional Intelligence was projected to put the mind of the people at ease.

If the people that are supposed to be revolting are busy finding new ways to build, repair, and reconstruct old and new connections with family and friends, then that would sway their minds off any form of revolt. Thus, the world capitalist system would now begin to look more caring, compassionate, and attentive to the problems of the masses. This is just another strategy which many believe would begin to fail sooner or later.

Now, there are two things involved with this so-called Emotional Intelligence. It's either Emotional Intelligence is the secret recipe that would make man extremely happy or it's the same old garbage that is just well repackaged in another form. In as much as many believed Emotional Intelligence goes in line with the former, others just believe Emotional Intelligence is nothing but the reincarnation of previous ideas that had refused to work in the past. Thus, it's only a matter of time before it fails.

Additionally, the control of one's emotions can be quite a curse more than a blessing. How? I'll tell you. When we are at the center of our emotions, when we know our left from right even at our weakest moments, and when we take control of our emotions no matter the circumstances or situation, we will be able to shield ourselves from making mistakes or even allowing our emotions control our decision-making skills. Now, this is a good thing.

But the curse comes when we now start developing the understanding of the feelings of others. We would be forced to act selfishly sometimes by using this trait to influence the decisions of others. Even if these decisions are great so long it doesn't favor us, we would still think of influencing the decisions. When this happens, we would realize that we have been making others do our bidding while neglecting theirs. We would find out we have been using our outstanding trait to exert an influence in the lives of others at the expense of their happiness. Now, this is a curse.

Also, there is no fine line between persuasion and manipulation. There is no fine line between influencing and brainwashing. Emotional Intelligence can be greatly misconstrued with respect to this definition. Now, if Emotional Intelligence can be misconceived this way, would you have said Emotional Intelligence is a good thing? Would you have vouched for the importance of this trait? Thus, there is no demarcation on how to properly wield the power of Emotional Intelligence.

While some people just believe persistence is the key to persuasion as regards Emotional Intelligence, others just believe Emotional Intelligence can be easily tainted with manipulation and brainwashing. If the tactics of persuasion don't work, they would just switch to force and manipulation. This is very evident in the world today. Little wonder why there are lots of brainwashed people around today. Persuasion deals with being intelligent and flexible, while manipulation deals with being rigid.

Others are also of the thought that Emotional Intelligence doesn't have anything to do with morality. As a matter of fact, it is very different from the realm of morality. No matter how hard you twist it, Morality and Emotional Intelligence are two diverse concepts which shouldn't be put together as two sides of the same coin.

When you are guided by the principles of morality, then you are able to define your Emotional Intelligence even better. But if you are not, you might easily get carried away by this outstanding trait, thereby, misusing its powers for your own selfish gain. Misguiding and motivating people wrongly would now be the best friend. This is where a lot of people with Emotional Intelligence end of being corrupt in the end. Without morality in it, one is bound to be corrupt.

This had been the major argument and believed to be the darkest side of Emotional Intelligence. If Emotional Intelligence can be guided, if Emotional Intelligence has it's own set of rules and regulations, if the use or Emotional Intelligence can be monitored or measured, and if the use of Emotional Intelligence can be greatly used, then there is nothing to be scared of. Emotional Intelligence would just be one hell of a powerful tool in reaching for greatness. Be that as it may, it is still as effective and efficient as ever even with its dark side. Thus, when used wrongly, Emotional Intelligence can be the most dangerous tool in the world.

The ability to control the feelings and decisions of others by being persuasive can be the most dangerous weapon one might need in order to reach the peak. This is why people of sound and great minds are being advised to only go into Emotional Intelligence. Whether we like it or not, we still can't stop anybody from harnessing this power. Remember, with great power comes great responsibility. But the question here is how can we be certain that the person wielding the power of Emotional Intelligence is of great mind? What if the persons are shallow thinkers that only see things their way?

Emotional Intelligence goes in line with being empathetic towards the feelings of others. According to Emotional Intelligence, when you show care for others in their moment of need, you are certainly building a pathway for yourself into that person's life. Thus, what is the assurance that our care and support we show to the people around us isn't just for our own selfish desire? Aside from this, the term manipulation and persuasion can be greatly misconstrued.

What is the assurance that you are being persuasive when in the real sense of the world, all your tactics are pointing towards manipulation? Additionally, people only make the word persuasion in order to paint their work as a good thing. And others might also tag you as a manipulator when they want people to think your work involves something bad. The bottom line is that people now use both words to suit themselves and give their explanations meaning. Even if you are good at persuasion, they would call you a manipulator if they don't like you and if you are a manipulator and extremely good at what you do, people won't see you for what you truly are.

Be that as it may, there is no such thing as purity without a blemish except the extraordinary. In as much as these controversies aren't really wrong, we can still call them the dark sides to Emotional Intelligence. Now, that doesn't mean Emotional Intelligence is totally bad. If you can control yourself and discipline your mind towards the thought of a greater good, then Emotional Intelligence is meant for you.

Chapter Ten

Does Emotional Intelligence Really Exist? (Now you know better)

I believe you know better as regards Emotional Intelligence, especially as we have discussed everything that you need to know about the subject matter. Many people still believe Emotional Intelligence does not really exist. Instead, they are of the opinion that our emotions are something we can't control, no matter how hard we try. Now, this is one place they always get it wrong. Emotional Intelligence does not refer to the control of our emotions directly but rather the control of the outcome as regards these emotions.

In other words, we can only hold control of our emotions via our own actions. If we end up holding our emotions intact without letting it influence our decisions, then we can say that we are being emotionally intelligent. Have you ever wondered why some people just act so mature no matter the circumstances? It is true that the older we get, the more we see life in a different dimension, however, not every old person has this ability and not every young person lacks it.

When you show everyone around you constantly how to

be a better person, no matter the circumstances, then you are definitely exhibiting the traits of Emotional Intelligence. Just like the saying goes, leaders aren't born, they are made - and so is Emotional intelligence in the real sense of the world. Many believe this ability is not something you are born with. Normally, an average human being is filled with all sorts of emotions running through the body.

From the regular emotions down to the crazy ones, each emotion depicts the feelings that are all boxed up inside the body. Now, nobody without the appropriate training or discipline can choose to forgo these emotions as they erupt out of us. In a situation where our emotions might take the better part of us, someone who is a master of their emotions would definitely react calmly and maturely. They would definitely use their heads ahead of their hearts.

In a situation where a diligent and hardworking employee just got sacked, a normal person would get extremely mad over the unfair treatment. No matter the excuse given by the organization, be it recession, retrenchment, or even resizing of their staff strength, you just won't get the drift. Your emotions would definitely get the better part of you. You would be forced to accept reality in the long run. But before then, you might have become a shadow of yourself.

A lot of people would fall back into their shell. They

would go into acute depression, thereby, shutting everybody out. To them, it would be like the whole world has gathered together just to be against them. When this happens, it would take the grace of God for us to be able to snap out of this mood sucking moments. Now, the question I would ask is this, why make yourself suffer by going through these particular kinds of torture? Why go through these heartbreaking moments when all you need to do is just to reconcile with the situation and make sure you stop letting your emotions take control?

Trust me, when we do this, our spiritual level will shoot up. Our relationships would thrive and see the new light. Our emotions would be tolerated even further. Our life would start taking good shape. Additionally, Emotional Intelligence goes in line with a perfect and sound body. Your body should be in a good working condition. That is the only way you can think with your head and instead of your heart. That is the only way you can keep your emotions in check.

I made an example with my own dad above as regards this point. An ailing body is a vulnerable one. When one gets sick and the body starts paving way for different kinds of illness, our emotions tend to get the better part of us. That is when we are most vulnerable. When my dad fell really sick, the same thing happened to him. He would easily snap at anyone in the room with him at the slightest mistake. He would get tensed at everything, no matter how little.

Like the master of Emotional Intelligence that I am, I already knew what to expect from the old man. I knew I had to be extra careful each time I was around him, but my siblings didn't know this and they became the victim of my father's emotional outbreaks. Now, after reading the chapters of this amazing book, would you really still come out boldly to say that Emotional Intelligence is just a myth? That it is just a fallacy?

Be that as it may, some people are of the opinion that the need for Emotional Intelligence is very crucial, especially with the rising societal issues that have sprung up in recent times. They believe Emotional Intelligence exists because of the solution it would proffer to these societal problems. If people can be more accommodating toward the emotions of others, and if we are also able to control our own emotions or the outcomes, as the case may be, then we will be able to move forward as one society.

That is an amazing concept of Emotional Intelligence. This explains why a lot of people don't mind paying large sums of money toward training themselves for a better version of themselves. What Emotional Intelligence does is to metamorphose someone from weak to strong, from needy to needed, and from average to intelligent. It would help develop your emotional skills and transform you from the average person you were yesterday to the intelligent person you will be later.

Others believe Emotional Intelligence does not really exist in the real sense because of its inability to be measured or even curtailed to an extent. There is absolutely no true measure or test of Emotional Intelligence rather than the fact that you stay neutral to the tribulations you find yourself in. Many believe that alone doesn't make you truly intelligent emotionally. Everybody can fake a nonchalant attitude to their emotions if the need arises. As desperate times call for desperate measures, so does this particular subject matter can be applied given the peculiarity of the situation. Thus, there is no big deal about it.

No matter how we turn this point, there is an atom of truth in it. If we can't truly come out to say we can measure this intelligence, then a mediocre person can come out today and start claiming the trait. Aside from this, I believe if you can say someone is intelligent in a particular field (mathematically, psychologically, sportsmanship, and so much more), so can you say someone who can perfectly control the outcome of their emotions is emotionally intelligent.

If a person is intelligent mathematically, that person would definitely excel in mathematics. Any questions bade of mathematics that are thrown toward him would be like throwing eggs on rocks. He would definitely solve them with no issues at all. This same instance applies to Emotional Intelligence. If one is emotionally intelligent, then he or she would definitely triumph in life. When life throws him or her different tribulations and obstacles, he or she will be able to sail past them swiftly and smoothly. In every sphere of life, an emotionally unintelligent person would definitely suffer as his or her emotions would lead the way each time in his or her affairs.

Finally, this argument has been going on for at least a decade with a lot of people rallying around both notions. If Emotional Intelligence really does exist, then does that mean every average person that can control their emotions or even fake it is emotionally intelligent? And if it doesn't exist, does that mean every leader out there that had been able to reach a lot of followers faked their Emotional Intelligence? If you can answer these questions correctly, then you should be able to tell if it exists or not.

Conclusion

I must say this had been one hell of a journey. From the beginning of this amazing book to the end, it had been an interesting journey which will definitely leave a mark in us. If you didn't know about Emotional Intelligence, well now you know better. Now you can do things in a much better form than the way you had done them before. Now you can approach things differently (calm and collected), unlike the way you had approached them before (emotional).

Without a doubt, I believe you now have a potential of managing and holding on to your old and new relationships. Nothing beats someone who has the whole world in his or her pockets. Now, how does one possesses that power? It's through Emotional Intelligence! When you have the power to turn every tide around and use them for your own benefit, people will always wonder if you are even human at all.

Remember, with great power comes great responsibility. Do not in any way misuse this outstanding power to manipulate or oppress anyone. What Emotional Intelligence teaches is to be compassionate and think of the greater good first. If you feel your relationships and connections are fading away, you know what to do. Instead of going back to your shell until someone fortunately comes along the line to build you back up, how about you check inward for a solution.

This is where unveiling your true and inner self comes into the picture. No one knows you better than yourself. Always make good use of this rare gift. Connect with your true self with the help of Spirituality. Go on a journey of discovering yourself and that will help you come back even stronger. Hold your values and principles tight. They would serve as the torch that would illuminate your path when you seem lost in your journey towards discovering yourself.

Now, go out there and make a difference. Go out there and show the world how much of the garbage you can take without flinching. As the saying goes, when life throws you a lemon, then make lemonade out of it. Any situation or circumstances you find yourself in, staying calm is of the essence. That would make you think ahead, and fast. You would be shocked at where the panacea would come from. Sometimes, it is our inability to be calm during tribulations that make us unable to see how close the solutions to the problems are.

Be that as it may, Emotional Intelligence can only be possible with the help of the 3Ps; patience, perseverance, and persuasion. If you can easily wield these three key weapons, then the rest will be history. You will be shocked at how great you would be, from your place of work to your home. Everything will fall into place. When your bosses start favoring you, others might think it's a fluke, not knowing its Emotional Intelligence that is working well for you.

Now, be the good person you have always been. Don't let this great power get to your head. And remember, absolutely power corrupts absolutely. Thanks for sticking with us all through our journey. You've been amazing. God bless and be Emotional Intelligent!

* * *

www.ingramcontent.com/pod-product-compliance
Lightning Source LLC
Chambersburg PA
CBHW070949080526
44587CB00015B/2247